Lake Monsters of Wisconsin

Lake Monsters of Wisconsin

By Chad Lewis

Foreword by Jerome Clark

On the Road Publications

Lake Monsters of Wisconsin

by Chad Lewis
Foreword by Jerome Clark

© 2016 On The Road Publications

All right reserved. No part of this publication may be produced or transmitted in any form or by any means, electrical or mechanical, including photocopy, recording, or any information storage or retrieval system with the permission in writing from the publisher.

ISBN: 978-0-9824314-7-4
Printed in the United States by Documation

On the Road Publications
3204 Venus Ave
Eau Claire, WI 54703
Email: chadlewis44@hotmail.com

Cover Design: Kevin Lee Nelson
Layout Design: Terry Fisk
Visuals:
Kevin Lee Nelson – The Fowler Lake Lop Jaw, The Lake Monona Sea Serpent, The Lake Ripley Fright, A Mystery in Lake Superior, Red Cedar Lake Monster.
Rick Fisk – The Denizen of Lake Koshkonong, The Lake Winnebago Water Beast, The Lake Delavan Giant, The Fox Lake Lurker.

Dedication

This book is dedicated to the great folklorist Charles E. Brown who spent many years collecting Wisconsin lake monster stories that would have been otherwise lost to all of us.

Table of Contents

Acknowledgments..i
Foreword..iii
Introduction vii

1. The Amphibious Demon of Brown's Lake............................. 1
2. Bozho – The Lake Mendota Sea Serpent.............................7
3. Cloverleaf Lakes Creature... 14
4. The Deadly Mississippi River Terror................................. 17
5. The Denizen of Lake Koshkonong................................... 22
6. The Elusive Beast of Lake Emerson..................................27
7. The Fowler Lake Lop Jaw..31
8. The Fox Lake Lurker.. 35
9. The Half Moon Monster..40
10. Jenny, The Monster of Geneva Lake................................ 48
11. The Lake Delavan Giant... 56
12. The Lake Hallie Whopper..62
13. The Lake Michigan Leviathan.. 66
14. The Lake Monona Sea Serpent....................................... 73
15. The Lake Ripley Fright...78
16. The Lake Waubesa What's It... 84
17. The Lake Winnebago Water Beast.................................. 87
18. The Long Neck of Long Lake... 95
19. The Monster in Devil's Lake... 99
20. A Mystery in Lake Superior.. 106
21. Pepie: The $50,000 Lake Monster.................................. 112
22. The Pewaukee Lake Intruder...119
23. Red Cedar Lake Monster.. 123
24. The Rock River Visitor..129
25. Rocky, The Rock Lake Terror....................................... 134
26. Even More Lake Monsters... 139

Bibliography.. 153
Author Bio.. 161

Acknowledgments

First and foremost, I would like to pay my respects to the wonderful researchers who came before me and paved the way for me to do an entire book on sea serpents including: Charles E. Brown, Brad Steiger, P.T. Barnum, Charles Fort, Jerome Clark, Loren Coleman, Patrick Huyghe, Bernard Heuvelmans, and A.C. Oudemans.

A giant thank you goes out to Noah Voss and Kevin Nelson—the most badass legend trippers on the face of the planet.

It is truly amazing that Jerome Clark agreed to write the foreword for this book. Over the last few years, I have been lucky enough to spark up a friendship with Jerome, and it is very inspiring to think that one of the true pioneers of this field is still sharing his expertise with the rest of us. Thanks Jerry!

All of the visual art was provided by the talented artists Rick Fisk and Kevin Lee Nelson.

Kevin Lee Nelson – The Front Cover, The Fowler Lake Lop Jaw, The Lake Monona Sea Serpent, The Lake Ripley Fright, A Mystery in Lake Superior, Red Cedar Lake Monster.

Rick Fisk – The Denizen of Lake Koshkonong, The Lake Winnebago Water Beast, The Lake Delavan Giant, The Fox Lake Lurker, The Half Moon Monster.

Another wonderful job of cleaning up this book was done by Sarah Szymanski.

Of course no adventure would be complete without Nisa Giaquinto and Leo Lewis—both of whom are the most interesting creatures out there.

Foreword

If this were the turn of the last century, the tales that follow in my friend Chad Lewis's wonderfully engaging book would have been called "snake stories," understood by Americans in those days to mean "tall tales from the provinces."

Snake stories welled up out of the culture in a colorful miscellany. Back then, newspaper accounts of lake monsters (as they're known, more precisely, in our time) borrowed the phrase "sea serpents"—which Lewis charmingly preserves in the text—from centuries of ocean-going reports of gigantic marine monsters. Lake monsters were ubiquitous, so much so that sightings were sometimes reduced to one-sentence summaries in brief news items from outlying districts in small-town weeklies. It was almost as if every lake was *expected* to harbor a sea serpent, there to be glimpsed now and then, usually at a distance, sometimes at terrifyingly close range.

These weren't the only snake stories, however. Immense snakes, sometimes alleged to be 100 feet long or more, prowled dry land, snatching up livestock and menacing hunters, farmers, and other humans. Both press accounts and folk tradition attested to hoop snakes, which took tail in mouth and rolled down the road in pursuit of their victims. They were said to be so venomous that if their fangs bit into a tree, the tree would wither and die within hours.

Foreword Jerome Clark

Even more alarmingly, dragon-like creatures, with or without wings, sometimes passed overhead, as sky (as opposed to mere sea) serpents. At the other extreme, persons suffering inexplicable gastro-intestinal disorders might learn one day that the cause was a snake that had taken up residence inside them, as often as not for years. And there were joint (aka glass) snakes, which if you struck them with a stick would break into pieces, only to reassemble themselves within minutes. As late as the early decades of the twentieth century, there was no surer way to spark a furious debate among newspaper readers than to print an editorial scoffing at hoop snakes and joint snakes.

The land, sky, and water of America—well, the same could be said of just about anywhere—all had (and have) their monsters, notorious and obscure. Today, if we are so inclined, we can speak with those who say they've seen them, as Chad Lewis has done repeatedly in his rambles. When we do that, we are exposed to genuinely puzzling testimony along with the more predictable errors in perception and lapses of sincerity. With the older accounts, on the other hand, we run up against the wild, woolly standards of provincial journalism, where invention sometimes began in the editorial office, the point being to entertain readers (who may have been privy to local jokes lost to us of later generations) or simply to fill space.

That doesn't explain every reported sighting of a lake monster (or other extraordinary anomaly) from another century, but it does make it harder to discern which ones we ought to take seriously. Still, it is surely significant that lake monsters have become far rarer critters than they were. Maybe that speaks to the professionalism of journalism since the early 1900s, when it got harder to make stuff up if you didn't have enough copy at hand. It is, at the same time, significant that lake monsters haven't *entirely* disappeared from native bodies of water. I am only one degree of separation from the lake monster observed a few years ago in a large South Dakota lake by my ex-wife and my older (adult) son. Only afterward did they learn that there has long been a local tradition that such a creature lives there, known to both American Indian and white residents of the area, but to virtually nobody else.

Foreword Jerome Clark

One doesn't have to believe—and I don't—that such animals are real in a biological sense, curiously leaving no bodies or other incontestable proofs of their presence, and moreover dwelling one at a time without mates or progeny. Their existence is in stories, memory, testimony. Once you've cleared away the mistakes, the jokes, and the hoaxes, what you're left with are people's vivid, very strange experiences, occurring in some liminal zone between the imaginary and the real, partaking—confoundingly—of elements of both without falling into one comfortable, familiar category or another.

Keep in mind that no clear picture of what a lake monster looks like emerges from the stories you're about to read. Some of the reports, I think you will agree, seem to have taken their inspiration from briefly glimpsed big but otherwise ordinary fish. Those aside, some describe creatures made up of random reptile parts (alligator jaws for one). There is, it needs to be stressed, precious little evidence that the early reports are of the standard, plesiosaur-like lake monsters of later decades. And even those are in a sense suspect, since in the twenty-first century paleontologists have a different understanding of what actual plesiosaurs were. They didn't resemble the Loch Ness monster, suffice it to say. The nineteenth-century lake monster of popular imagination and occasional sighting was a huge snake, a literal serpent.

So imagination plays a role in all of this on both ends, from informant (witness) to messenger (media), but we already knew that. Maybe the aspect of the imaginary just makes things more weird, because it suggests that imagination cannot be contained solely within our heads, our dreams, our fictions. Maybe there are times when it escapes into the experienceable world, and what then? Well, then, all kinds of things can be encountered; however one defines "encountered," it can't help removing—contrary to every complacent assumption we have about how we interact with the world—experience from event.

Events happen in consensus reality, and they are documentable, or anyway potentially so. When no longer synonymous with events, experiences can be quite something else, real enough to play out in front of more than one

Foreword Jerome Clark

person at a time (and thus not a hallucination in any prosaic sense) but sufficiently unreal to endure in nothing but memory and testimony. Unable to pigeon-hole such phenomena, we shrug and call them legends and anecdotes, and if they truly offend us, we make life as unpleasant as possible for those who report such heretical visions and encounters. Ridicule is the bluntest of instruments. We're good at silencing unwelcome testimony, but not at giving it a hearing and seeking to come to grips with it.

Therefore be grateful that the world produces the occasional admirable soul like Chad Lewis, whose relentless curiosity takes him where the timid dare not tread. To be Chad Lewis, you have to possess an open—which is not the same as a vacant—mind and to respect what people have to tell you.

If they're coherent and (to every appearance) earnest, moreover, you don't have to put words into their mouths so that you can "explain" everything. And if they tell you they've experienced a fantastic creature such as a lake monster, and if misperception of an ordinary animal or object is unlikely under the given circumstances, you don't have to dismiss their testimony just because conclusive proof, or even very good evidence, of aquatic unknowns has never been demonstrated. After all, if the world is finite, experience is boundless. As the old maps used to say, here there be dragons.

—Jerome Clark
July 6, 2016

Introduction

It is time for the classic images of Wisconsin—namely cheese, beer, and crazy Green Bay Packers fans—to step aside and make room on the notoriety mantle for lake monsters. As you are about to discover, nowhere else in the U.S. can lay claim to such an abundance of lake monster legends. In fact, there are so many tales of creatures dwelling in the lakes, rivers, and streams that Wisconsin has now emerged as the Lake Monster Capital of America.

Stories of these creatures permeate the entire state: from the rural secluded fishing lakes of the Northwoods, to the southern lakes filled with Chicago tourists, and to the spacious waters of the Great Lakes. As the human population continues to exponentially grow and spread, more and more of our natural habitat gets destroyed in the process, leaving a scant amount left over for legends to survive. What happens to that howling banshee said to haunt the old woods when the woods are demolished to make room for a parking lot? This is what makes sea serpent legends so fascinating—lakes and rivers might just serve as a last bastion where undiscovered mysteries can not only survive, but flourish.

Introduction Chad Lewis

Lake monsters have long been a favorite research area of mine. For years, I traveled the world in search of what was left of the famed sea monsters. I have been on two expeditions to Loch Ness to search out the world's best known serpent—Nessie. I shared pints of Guinness with locals as I searched for Ireland's Lough Ree monster. Research excursions in the United States brought me to Lake Erie, Flathead Lake, and dozens of other locations around the country in my all-out quest to find these still undiscovered beasts. It seems a bit ironic that after so many years of traveling the world in search of lake monsters, I would discover that my home state of Wisconsin is ground zero.

As you will undoubtedly notice, this book does not contain a final chapter on conclusions, one which would offer answers to these perplexing legends. The exclusion of this chapter was purposefully done for two reasons. First, I have made comments and given my thoughts on each individual case when I deemed it necessary. But more importantly, I wanted these legends and stories to stand on their own. Of course, I could have gone on *ad nauseam* about how these monsters may actually be misidentified logs or large sturgeon; I could have spelled out the intricacies of lateral waves. None of these wild speculations would have conclusively solved any of these legends. I have come to believe that perhaps the treasure doesn't come from assigning flimsy answers to these questions, but rather from the imagination and sense of wonder they stimulate in each of us. Of course, it would be a gigantic scientific breakthrough to discover a previously unknown species, or re-discover one believed to be long extinct, yet, conversely, it also brings a smile to my face to think that 100 years from now children might still be hesitant to dangle their feet into these waters due to these monster stories. So grab your snorkeling gear, load up the fishing boat, or just simply relax on the beach and explore these legends. After your adventure you might just discover that the weirdest and most interesting thing out there is you.

Keep an eye out...

—Chad Lewis

The Amphibious Demon of Brown's Lake

Where To Encounter It

Brown's Lake is located right outside of Burlington. The lake has a boat landing, a public beach, and several businesses which provide perfect monster hunting starting points.

Creature Lore

Imagine waking up, flipping open your local newspaper, and seeing the story headline, "An Aquatic or Amphibious Demon." For those in 1876 who were reading the August 10th edition of the *Burlington Standard*, no such imagination was needed, because the paper included every minute detail of this sensational monster encounter.

Most of what we know of this case comes from a Dear Editor letter to the newspaper in which a terrified witness recalled the "God's Truth" about

Lake Monsters of Wisconsin

a week long camping expedition that turned into a puzzling brush with the unknown. On the evening of July 30th, the writer and his friend were sitting upon a bank of the lake when they both spotted something "like a log twenty feet long" floating along the water about 100 feet away from the north point of the island. Having never seen a log maneuver in such a manner before, the men quickly followed their collective curiosity and called out to a nearby boater for assistance. When the "expert oarsman" reached the island, the two men discovered that they were not the only ones who had encountered the unknown beast. The boater told of two other men fishing just south of the island that had also just seen a similar creature swimming in the rushes. Together, the make shift search party quickly set off in hopes of solving the bizarre mystery—only to discover that the elusive beast was nowhere to be found.

The next morning (August 1st), one of the men was out collecting fire wood when he came rushing back into camp "pale and exhausted from fright" telling the tale of "seeing the very old devil in the rushes." Filled with excitement, and barely able to spill out the details, the man told of seeing something "as big as an elephant" rush towards the island with "fearful velocity." The terrified witness was able to gather a close look at the 30-foot creature and claimed it was "a fish as large as a barrel and as long as a barn." To make the identification even more puzzling, the creature was said to have eyes "like fire and as large as pumpkins." Perhaps spooked by something unseen, the creature made a tremendous splash and "strode out" for deeper water, quickly disappearing from sight.

On Friday the 4th, before sunrise, the camp was awakened by "a rumbling noise and frightful splashing" in the water that resembled the noise produced by "rolling saw logs in quick succession down a steep bank into the lake." The startled, sleepy-eyed campers rushed down to the lake just in time to see the giant beast swimming away from the shore on the surface of the water leaving a large wake "not unlike that of an old side-wheel steamboat." What they had just witnessed was unlike anything else they

The Amphibious Demon of Brown's Lake

Artist's rendition of the creature
(Courtesy of the Burlington Press Standard)

had ever seen, estimating the creature to be over 27 feet in length, with a circumference of 5 ½ to 6 feet. But instead of being the size and shape of a typical serpent, this beast seemed more like something created by Dr. Frankenstein. The giant's broad, flattened head occupied nearly ¼ of its body, and adding to its fierce look, the beast had "tremendous under jaws projecting 12 to 16 inches" filled with razor sharp incisors. The hodge-podge of body parts continued with its tail, which was described as being the size of its head and covered with a triple fin. It also had pectoral feet and two large and boney ventral fins. The deep, glossy green color of the beast faded into "blue on the sides and a dirty yellow below."

Later that afternoon, a group of ladies leisurely swimming on the north end of the island got the scare of a lifetime. Rushing wildly into the men's camp, the women began screaming and crying about having "been chased out of the water" by a "Herculean Saurian" who followed them "some 50 feet up the steep bank," before coiling 25 feet into the air and plunging back into the safety of the water. Frantic with fear, and praising God for their narrow escape from death, the women adamantly proclaimed their vow to never again set foot in Brown's Lake.

Lake Monsters of Wisconsin

The strange letter to the editor seems to serve as a public service warning, meant to protect the unknowing community from the three deadly serpents inhabiting Brown's Lake. If the ultimate goal was to scare off potential visitors to the lake, the local newspaper was buying none of it. As an editorial rebuttal to the camper's letter, the newspaper wrote:

> We trust our readers will not lose much sleep on account of this 'monster of the deep' as we verily believe it is nothing else than the 'Mammoth Pickeral' first seen by Mr. William Hockers full a twenty-five years ago. He has seen it several times since—and once came near capturing it.

All of the mystery and intrigue surrounding the lake only added to the public's fascination with the story, and soon the lakeshore was overflowing with curious sight seekers looking for their own sighting of the monster—regardless of its true identity. One such visitor was George Sherwood, who, while strolling along the shoreline in search of beastly footprints, had his opera glasses stolen from his horse and buggy. Sherwood was on a monster quest to discover the beast, and not having his opera glasses would make it difficult to scan the entire lake, so Sherwood placed the following ad in the local paper:

> If the party who stole the opera glasses out of my carriage at Brown's Lake last Thursday would rather have $5, he can return the glasses and receive the above reward. No questions asked and avoid trouble.

It is not known if the monster spotting opera glasses were ever returned, but several others in the community were able to catch sight of the beast—sans glasses.

In 1956, the *Racine Journal Times* published an article that might lend some credence to those who believed the monster was merely a misidentified large fish. The article told of a crew of seven men who began netting the lake with hopes of ridding it of its large carp, which they described as being nothing more than a "menace to fish life" and aquatic life.

The Amphibious Demon of Brown's Lake

Even with good intentions, it appears the brave seven men failed to best the menace, because during my research into this case, I spoke with a lot of people who claimed to have seen large carp while fishing out on the lake, but not one person mentioned any large pickerel fish (the original theory). Many that I spoke with expressed skepticism that a lake monster was currently calling the lake home, others scoffed, and a few even laughed heartily at the idea. Yet, I did speak with several locals who, throughout the years, had heard whisperings of the lake legend, yet no one was able to add any new specifics.

A beautiful day at Brown's Lake

In 1976, celebrating the one-hundred-year anniversary of the monster sightings, *the Burlington Standard* revisited the story for an August 9 article. They interviewed several lakeside residents who claimed to have never heard anything about the legend. However, unlike my research, they did eventually turn up one individual who not only believed in the beast, but had devised a theory to explain its 140-year elusiveness. The newspaper talked with Marshall Petrie, a life-long area resident who grew up hearing tales of the Brown's Lake monster. Stories so bizarre that they propelled him on a lifelong mission to research the history and mystery

Lake Monsters of Wisconsin

of the lake. One odd natural phenomenon is that it contains a curiously large hole in the center of the north quarter. The length of the mysterious hole extends to nearly 1 ½ acres, and it was once thought to be bottomless. Petrie claimed that when the first sound recordings of the hole were attempted, the bottom was simply beyond reach. As kids, Petrie and his brother, Mort, dropped a bundle of rope down the hole, finally reaching bottom at 100 feet. Over the years, the giant hole has shrunk considerably, leaving scientists to believe it is being filled in with silt. However, Petrie believed that it was the giant monster who was responsible for the depth change, as the beast uses the giant hole for its sleeping and hiding quarters. Perhaps someday the monster will once again leave its lair and return to the business of scaring lakeside campers.

Bozho: The Lake Mendota Sea Serpent

Where to Encounter It

Lake Mendota is located near the University of Wisconsin – Madison, forked by Highways 151 and 113. The lake can be easily accessed through numerous locations, including Marshall Park, Warner Park, Tenney Park, and Governor Nelson State Park. The sightings have occurred throughout the entire lake.

Creature Lore

Any good sea serpent researcher has to be wary of regular lake items being misidentified as some unknown sea monster. It sometimes happens that those unfamiliar with a lake's behavior may suddenly believe that an everyday occurrence is actually caused by some supernatural force. The most common culprits for these alleged sightings tend to be floating logs, tipped over boats, waves, swimmers, rocks, other fish, and even other animals. On the flipside of this are those skeptical witnesses who originally thought they were viewing these normal lake objects, only to observe the "objects" come to life and rear their huge head and bodies from the water. In the waters of Lake Mendota, it seems there may be more sea serpents than logs.

The American Indians were the first people to dread encountering the beast of Lake Mendota, but it was the white settlers who ultimately gave the sea serpent the moniker "Bozho." Folklorist Charles E. Brown believed that the name "Bozho" was an abbreviated version an Indian hero or God called Winnebozho. Oral legends tell of the giant serpent taking a shower bath in the lake, an action that was thought responsible for the whirling waterspouts that formed over the lake.

One of the earliest sightings in Lake Mendota occurred during the 1860s. In his book, *The W-Files*, researcher Jay Rath wrote about the strange experience of W.J. Park and his wife while boating near Governor's Island. The couple was out on a leisurely row around the lake when they pulled up next to what they believed was a floating log. When Park lifted his oar up to smack the log, the water erupted and the "log" dove under the water. Park was convinced that he and his wife had seen a genuine lake monster, but fearing ridicule, the couple kept the encounter to themselves. It wasn't until many other serpent sightings began to circulate that he finally decided to share his bizarre sighting with others.

June in Madison meant that the town would be bustling with tourists looking to escape to the lake for their family vacations. It was also the busiest time of year for Billy Dunn, who was one of Madison's most infamous fishermen. In 1892, the *Chicago Daily Tribune* recapped Dunn's sensational 1883 encounter with the deadly water monster. According to the newspaper, this is how it happened. Dunn and his wife were out fishing

Bozho: The Lake Mendota Sea Serpent

Chicago Tribune illustration of Dunn's battle

near what was called Livesey's Bluff, when he noticed a black object "moving threateningly towards the boat." As the creature approached, Dunn was able to discern the outline of a large snake as it rose up several feet out of the water. "The forked tongue darting fiercely backwards and forwards," as it mashed its way through the disturbed water. The experienced fisherman was not intimidated as he seized his oar and braced for the attack. The serpent, with a "fierce hiss" shot upon the boat and was quickly greeted by Dunn's trusty oar. Instinct took over and the serpent clamped its "long black fangs" down through the wooden oar . As the beast tried to thrash itself from the entanglement, Dunn swiftly grabbed his side holstered hatchet and began smashing "blow after blow" down on the serpent. Bloodied and beaten, the snake released itself from the oar and sank under the water. Dunn stated that he did not trust himself enough to guess at the length of the monster, yet he did say that "it was of a light greenish color and covered with white spots." My favorite part of this fascinating story is that Dunn was said to have kept the oar, which still had

Lake Monsters of Wisconsin

a couple of long black fangs imbedded into it, as a trophy of sorts, reminding him of his victorious battle with Lake Mendota's sea monster. Whatever became of that oar is not known.

If you were a sea serpent hunter back in 1892, there would have been no better place for you to conduct your research than Madison's Lake Mendota. On July 25, the *Oshkosh Daily Northwestern* briefly mentioned, "Not long ago a sea serpent was seen in Lake Mendota." It must have been a very busy news day because the article left out all of the pertinent details of the sighting. On August 30, the *Marshfield Times* reported, "Another sea serpent had been seen in Lake Mendota." Once again, the newspaper failed to give specific details of the encounter. Luckily, just over a week later, another more descriptive encounter took place. It was October 6 when local monster hunter John Schott began an organized hunt for what the *Janesville Gazette* called "the slimy denizen of the deep." Schott, who had already encountered the creature on three different occasions, described the creature, stating, "It has a large head, flat on top and square like a box." He claimed that the creature's head stood a good three feet out of the water and was connected to a large 25-foot body, which was partially submerged. Three weeks later, another group of men would corroborate Schott's size estimates. The day was October 28, and the chilly winds of the season had begun to set in when a number of young men braved the harsh fall conditions and set out sailing. Midway through the route, the dozen sailors caught a good view of a huge serpent moving through the water. *The Eau Claire News* wrote, "All of them declare that it was very large. Some say it is was fully 35 feet long, others say 30, and the lowest estimate is 25 feet. Not being on a hunt for the serpent they had no firearms and were glad to escape from the monster."

In August of 1899, a group of women were enjoying a relaxing camping expedition along the beautiful banks of the lake. The camping party consisted of Mrs. E. Grove, Mrs. J.J. Pecher, and several additional unnamed women. To help alleviate the effects of the summer heat, the party jumped

Bozho: The Lake Mendota Sea Serpent

in their boat and headed out on the cool, refreshing lake. Suddenly, the women noticed something bobbing up out of the water. According to the *Racine Daily Journal*, the women "saw a long, snake-like monster with a head ten inches across, and a tail which had horns." The group was not willing to risk their lives on the hopes of the good intentions of the beast, so they frantically paddled for the safety of the shore. The commotion of their paddling evidently scared the creature, which abruptly plunged back into the depths of the lake, creating "a great deal of foam," along with it. Following up on the women's story, the *Wisconsin State Journal* skeptically reported that the six-foot long monster was equipped with two three-inch horns protruding from its tail. The women were not alone in their sighting. That same month another witness saw the monster. The story was summarized in Jay Rath's book, *The W-Files*, and tells of Barney Reynolds, who caught sight of a similar creature near the landing for the Bernard Boat Yard. It is unknown whether both sightings were of the same creature.

In 1942, Charles E. Brown of the Wisconsin Folklore Society put out a monograph titled *Sea Serpents* detailing Wisconsin's sea serpent past. In the monograph, he devotes the first entry to the many sightings of Bozho. Brown did an amazing job at capturing some essential Wisconsin sightings. One of the later sightings occurred in 1917, when a University of Wisconsin student was enjoying the beach area of Picnic Point on the north shore when they stumbled upon what looked like a fish scale. Curious, the student brought the tough scale to his professor who determined that the scale came from the body of a sea serpent. This sensational scale story opened the door for others to report their own odd sightings in the lake. Brown wrote that later in the year a fisherman was trying his luck at a perch off the end of Picnic Point. At a distance of 100 feet out, he spotted a "large snake-like head, with large jaws and blazing eyes emerge from the deep water." The sight was so overwhelming that the man could do nothing but stare at the creature, his own body unwilling to react. Eventually, the man pulled himself together and fled from the shoreline, leaving

Lake Monsters of Wisconsin

both his pole and basket behind. Hoping to find an explanation to his sighting, the man shared the account with several of his friends, "but no one believed his story."

Brown's odd collection of Lake Mendota stories ranged from the previous scary encounter to this more humorous tale of a young lady who discovered that the creature was a little too friendly for her liking. Not too long after the abovementioned story, a couple of university students were basking in the sun at the end of a frat house pier. The young man and his female companion were lying face down, letting the sun soak in through their backs. After a few moments, the girl felt something tickling the sole of her foot. Convinced that her friend was the culprit, the woman glanced over at him only to find his eyes were closed in relaxation. The woman brushed off the incident and began to relax. However, a few moments later the tickling resumed, and this time the woman spun over quickly and saw

Plenty of room for a monster to hide

Bozho: The Lake Mendota Sea Serpent

"the head and neck of a huge snake, or dragon" extended above the water. The woman reported that it "had a friendly, humorous look in its big eyes." The creature had been using its long tongue to caress the feet of the sunbathing girl. She quickly grabbed her friend, and they scurried back to the safety of the frat house.

Brown also included several less detailed stories of the serpent overturning canoes, chasing sailboats, and frightening bathers. He wrote that for the most part this serpent was "a rather good-natured animal," whose pranks were basically harmless. Brown also made the distinction between these mischievous serpent sightings and the more sinister "old Indian water spirits, long-tailed, horned, cat-like animals believed to have a den in the deep water of Governor's Island on the north shore of the lake."

With so many credible sightings taking place, one could easily wonder why no hard evidence of the creature has been found. Lake Mendota has been called the most studied lake in America and even contains a remote sensor buoy in its waters used by the University of Wisconsin, and during the summer, the lake is highly used by an assortment of people. You would think that the commotion of the boaters, swimmers, and those fishing would stir up these large creatures, yet year after year goes by without so much as a hint of a credible sighting. Skeptics claim that the reported sea serpents were nothing more than a pickerel or garfish with a head full of fishing lures scaring all the naïve tourists. Regardless of the explanation, the mystery of Lake Mendota continues on. Maybe someday someone will find Billy Dunn's fang-filled oar, and the mystery can be solved once and for all. Until that day comes, grab your bait and head over to Lake Mendota.

Cloverleaf Lakes Creature

Where To Encounter It

The Cloverleaf Lakes are made up of Pine, Grass, and Round Lakes of northern Wisconsin near Clintonville. Several roads circle the lakes along with several businesses along the shores that provide for good monster hunting headquarters.

Creature Lore

By 1910, while most sea serpent stories throughout the country were rapidly fading out, the Creature of Cloverleaf Lakes was just emerging as a puzzling new legend. As far as we know, the creature only appeared for a very limited time before disappearing back into the depths of the water forever. The limited amount of information we have on this case comes from a series of newspaper articles from 1910 that pronounce the arrival of the Cloverleaf Lakes creature.

Residents of Clintonville must have felt a ping of caution when they picked up the August 22, 1910 edition of the *Janesville Daily Gazette* and

Cloverleaf Lakes Creature

read that a "strange beastie" was patrolling the Cloverleaf Lakes, and the beast had been seen by upwards of eight people. Residents who owned cottages along the lakes described being frightened by a six-foot-long mysterious creature with "long claws." The fearfulness of the residents was explained further by the *Eau Claire Leader*, which warned that several citizens from around the lake "narrowly escaped" their encounter with the hideous monster. One would assume that any near-death scenario in the water would have warranted a full story—but these encounters must have just been too scary to print because the article lacks any further details of the sightings.

The paper did, however, include the story of two women who were out enjoying a beautiful day on the lake when the unidentified monster began chasing after their boat. Once again, the newspaper failed to include any more details on the strange encounter. I think it is safe to assume that the women survived their creepy ordeal since the story did make it to the paper.

Looking to personalize the growing legend, the *Janesville Daily Gazette* wrote that the beast had even been seen by a prominent citizen of the area, a Mr. William Schrander, City Treasurer for Clintonville. Of course, no additional details of his sighting were given either, but attaching respectable people to the list of serpent witnesses often provided instant credibility to the sightings.

> **Strange "Beastie" That Crawls or Swims, With Huge Paws and Frightens People.**

Article headline in the Janesville Gazette

Lake Monsters of Wisconsin

What makes this case truly unique is that not only had the beast been seen swimming in the lake, but it also apparently had the ability to use its large claws to easily maneuver about along the lake bottom as well. The description of a six-foot-long beast with huge paws and long claws does bring up the possibility that the people of the Cloverleaf Lakes area were simply witnessing an alligator and not a genuine sea serpent. Further credibility to the alligator theory was given by the *Janesville Daily Gazette* which claimed that "a baby alligator was turned loose in the lakes some years ago and the supposed sea serpent may be this reptile." Believe it or not, stories of alligators being captured in Wisconsin are not that uncommon. There are hundreds of accounts of these giant reptiles being hauled out of our waterways. However, there is a huge drawback to the theory of alligators being the root of sea serpent stories: these cold blooded creatures would have a very difficult time surviving one harsh Wisconsin winter, much less the lengthy lifespan of these legends.

As far as we know the Cloverleaf Lakes sightings only lasted a couple of weeks, thereby increasing the possibility that it was nothing more than a misplaced alligator that was terrifying the locals. Since no sea creature or alligator was ever captured, this case looks to remain unsolved.

Three connected lakes provide plenty of hiding spots

The Deadly Mississippi River Monster

Where to Encounter It

The numerous miles of the Mississippi shoreline provide countless opportunities for you to catch a glimpse of the water serpent. Many of the sightings originated near La Crosse.

Creature Lore

Although this book is filled with tales of numerous monsters lurking in lakes, with multiple tributaries, miles and miles of roaming space, and plenty of prey, rivers might just be the perfect breeding ground for serpents. If rivers are indeed the ideal location for monsters, then no river would make a better suited home than the 2,300 mile Mississippi River. In addition to Pepie, the river is believed to be home to several other serpents as well.

In the late 1800s and early 1900s, many resorts littered the riverbanks of the Mississippi, providing campers and vacationers with waterfront cottages and campsites. For decades, early pioneers of La Crosse often told

Lake Monsters of Wisconsin

harrowing tales of close encounters with some bizarre aquatic serpent. This unknown beast was sighted up and down the Mississippi from La Crosse, Wisconsin to Dresbach, Minnesota.

In the summer of 1901, the *La Crosse Daily Press* told of another "hair breadth" escape from the "poisonous creature." This encounter began during a hot July morning as a party enjoying a day out on the river decided to pull ashore for lunch. As one of the gentleman was enjoying his lunch from the safety of shore, a large snake-like creature "which had been coiled around a huge log" slipped off into the river, "hissing like escaping steam." The monster's greenish black body also had splotches of white near its neck, yet the most puzzling part came from the two large horns—like those of a calf—that adored the beast's head. Much like all the previous sightings, the physical description of the creature did not match those of any surrounding wildlife. Unfortunately, the witness didn't have much time complete the beast's identity because the monster quickly thrashed its tail, turning the nearby water into foam, before it disappeared into the depths of the Mississippi. Needless to say, the party took little time in locating another place to calm their nerves and enjoy their lunch.

While the abovementioned unknown monster was never caught, other known monsters have often been pulled from the river, as evidenced by the 1902 story covered by the *Eau Claire Weekly Telegram*. On a bright August day, fisherman Edward Clark was out on the river when his sturdy angling line quickly went taut. Whatever was lurking on the other end of his line was so powerful that it began to drag the boat through the water as though it was nothing more than a small piece of driftwood. Not knowing exactly what type of monster was dangling just beneath the surface, Clark was surprised to see a gigantic sturgeon rear its head above water. After lugging the boat over two miles, the beast, exhausted from exertion, finally gave up the fight and was landed. The massive sturgeon stretched out over six feet two inches in length and weighed in at 115 pounds, prompting the newspaper to declare that it was the "largest fish" ever taken from the upper Mississippi River.

The Deadly Mississippi River Monster

In the summer of 1904, a mysterious anomaly was pulled from the river by Oscar Millard, a local clam fisherman. According to the *Elyria Reporter* the Frankenstein-like monster resembled "a long-eared dog with six webbed feet and fins like a fish." Curiously, the newspaper also claimed the beast "was equipped with the tail of a fish and had a head shaped much like a walrus." Obviously puzzled by the creature the paper ended the story by stating that "nothing like it has ever been seen here before."

A few weeks later, another startling report from a Mississippi River ferry worker caught the attention of the local community. Samuel Cummings, a river crossing official the *Eau Claire Leader* described as an "authority" on all things river, believed that a "huge unknown nameless fish" or sea serpent was patrolling the waters around La Crosse. Working everyday on the river, Cummings would certainly be all too familiar with the local wildlife and fish, yet the beast swimming in the Mississippi was far bigger than anything he had ever encountered. Looking to explain how such a gigantic beast could have found its way into the river, the ferryman believed that the fish must have made its way up from the Gulf of Mexico.

Mr. Cummings may have been onto something with his beliefs, because one of today's leading theories contends that these mysterious beasts were once ocean dwellers who happened to swim up river, only to find themselves trapped. Or perhaps these creatures simply found the Mississippi River to their liking and decided to stay—permanently. If the latter is the case, they certainly would not be alone, as for the past few decades numerous species from the bull shark to the Asian carp have been slowly inching their way up river.

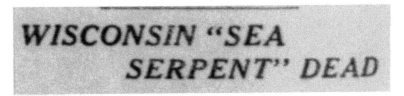

1910 Dubuque Telegraph Herald article headline

Lake Monsters of Wisconsin

In 1910, an article in the *Dubuque Telegraph Herald* proclaimed that Wisconsin's sea serpent was "dead." The paper reported on the discovery of the carcass of a giant five-foot long gar fish that was rotting on the shores near Trempealeau. Fishermen in the area believed that the creature was a "baby whale or alligator," as something large had been terrorizing the community for several months.

In 1921, the sea monster legends were once again in full bloom along with Mississippi. This time it was the *La Crosse Tribune* that spark up the interest by reporting on several serpent sightings that occurred on the north side of La Crosse. Since witnesses reported that the beast was seen swimming in a southern direction, the newspaper facetiously wrote that it had consulted with several mathematicians who predicted the monster would arrive in the southern end of town within a few days. No descriptions of the beast were provided.

During the late 1800s and early 1900s sightings of these aquatic beasts set off a firestorm of controversy; both experts and laypersons alike scrambled to come to grips with just exactly what witnesses were seeing. Skeptics tried to explain away all sightings as misidentifications, hoaxes, or complete delusion on the part of the observers. At the same time, those who actually laid eyes on these beasts held firm in their belief that what they saw did not fit easily into any known classification. Thanks to the fantastical stories of the local newspapers, which warned of giant man-eating fish patrolling the Mississippi waters, protective parents forbade their children from playing near the river. Evidence of the killer fish was soon provided when several recovered bodies of drowning victims actually had what appeared to be claw and scratch marks around their ankles and calves. The belief was that these unsuspecting victims were out fishing or swimming in the river, when the serpent latched onto their legs and dragged them out to their watery graves.

The Deadly Mississippi River Monster

The La Crosse section of the river is a hotbed of sightings

Thankfully, the long held fear and avoidance of the river has mostly subsided over the years. Today the Mississippi is a hopping place for fishing, hiking, boating, camping, and recreation. Many of the serpent legends and cautionary tales of the river have all been nearly forgotten—yet every time I am in the Mississippi River, I can't help but imagine that each piece of driftwood or rogue tree branch that brushes up against my legs is actually the long tentacles of some killer serpent just waiting to drag me to my death.

The Denizen of Lake Koshkonong

Where To Encounter It

Lake Koshkonong is just east of the town of Koshkonong. The lake has a public beach, nature area and boat landings for your monster viewing.

Creature Lore

Many of the sea monsters in this book are of a size that dwarfs any known species inhabiting the bodies of water where they are said to dwell, giving the impression that all lake monsters are of gigantic size. Yet, when you consider the fact that the maximum depth of Lake Koshkonong is only 7 feet, the monster seen here must have been considerably smaller that its contemporaries—even though the lake's 10,000-acre size would provide plenty of room for a long thin creature to roam about.

In their book, *Wisconsin Lore*, Robert Gard and L.G. Sorden tell of a American Indian superstition that revolved around the fear of something deadly waiting in Lake Koshkonong. The legend tells of the first Native people having a healthy respect for the lake due to the giant monster that was said to attack anyone foolish enough to test their luck. In fact, it was

The Denizen of Lake Koshkonong

said that "all who attempted it were sure to be drowned." One cautionary story involves two Potawatomi brothers who scoffed at the serpent legend, believing it was complete fabrication, and set out to prove it to their fellow tribesmen. In a test of bravery (or foolishness) the brothers launched their canoes in opposite directions in order to navigate the entire lake, while the rest of the nervous tribe anxiously watched from the safety of dry land. Throughout the day, Natives in camp were fearful that the lake creature would gobble up the men for its next meal, so they sang sacred protection songs hoping to ensure the brothers' safe return. Soon a fierce wind began whipping through camp and as darkness began settling in, there was still no sign of the brothers. The next day, the tribe's fears were realized when the brother's empty capsized canoes washed ashore. Although no one bore witness to the accident, it was immediately known that the deadly monster of lake had struck again. A few days later, the brothers' decomposing bodies were discovered by several white men who observed white clay caked in the men's ears and nostrils—a sign the Natives took as definitive proof that the monster of the lake had drowned them.

On a cold November day in 1887, weirdness decided to make another appearance at Lake Koshkonong. Two duck hunters, A. I. Sherman of Fort Atkinson, and Charles Bartlett of Milwaukee, were out enjoying the day. The friends were busily rowing their boat, when off at a distance of 150 feet, something strange caught their attention. The shocked pair watched as a giant snake-like creature moved quickly towards the center of the lake. As the creature swam, it kept its head a good two feet out of the water. From their vantage point, the men could make out another 10 feet or so of the creature's half-submerged trunk, all of which was estimated to be about eight inches thick. Using the beast's large wake on the calm water as a calculation of its dimensions, the witnesses estimated the overall size of the beast to be about 30-40 feet.

Fascinated by the mysterious creature, curiosity quickly overtook the hunters as they began furiously rowing toward the beast with the intent of solving this mystery, regardless of whether it meant capturing the beast

Lake Monsters of Wisconsin

or simply killing it. Yet their plans were soon thwarted when the creature—either spooked by the commotion or simply possessing an uncanny sense of danger—quickly slipped back under the surface of the water. By the time the story was reported in the November 19 edition of the *Oshkosh Daily Northwestern*, the mysterious creature had inexplicably grown to sixty feet in size, a common side effect caused by the telling and retelling of a sea serpent sighting.

Wisconsin folklorist Charles Brown wrote about several strange sightings in the lake for his *Sea Serpents* monograph. The first told of a pair of grizzled old carp fishermen who were out on the lake working their nets when something very large made its way toward them. Frozen in amazement, the men watched as a large beast swam by and ripped apart all of their nets. Judging by the way the creature fiercely twisted, thrashed, and turned in rage, the men were convinced that they were not dealing with any known fish—at least not one that either of them had ever encountered.

Fishermen often encountered the beast

The Denizen of Lake Koshkonong

Does a killer monster still lurk here?

Another tale was that of an old farmer living on the west side of the lake who regularly watered his pigs along the lakeshore. The farmer was certain that several of his missing pigs were actually snatched up and devoured by the lake monster.

Brown also mentions several sightings of a large unknown creature off the mouth of the Koshkoning (Koshkonong) Creek, yet no further details were provided—leaving us with the task of using our imaginations to fill in all the fanciful details.

Some 70 years after the intrepid Brown sought out the creature, I found myself following in his footsteps as I spent several days interviewing locals of the area with the hope of finding someone who had a recent sighting or first-hand encounter with the lake monster. After numerous interviews and countless dead ends, my optimism soon ran dry. When no witnesses could be found, I turned to the Hoard Historical Museum (the local history museum). If any additional stories of the monster survived, it was a good bet that the historical society would have them on file. Unfortunately, they too were curiously surprised to learn of the lake's sordid creature past. With no known modern day reports, it is far too easy to

Lake Monsters of Wisconsin

brush off the early sightings as being nothing more than a misidentified pickerel or sturgeon—simply a giant fish that was inflated through the eyes of mistaken witnesses. Yet deep down, my hope is that whatever creature terrorized the lake one hundred years ago is still out there waiting, watching, and yearning for some foolish daredevil to launch their canoe.

The Elusive Beast of Lake Emerson

Where to Encounter It

Lake Emerson (Humbird Pond) is located in Humbird. The lake has a public boat landing, beach area, and county park to watch for the beast.

Creature Lore

Just when most sea serpent stories from around the world were dying out, the legend of Lake Emerson's beast was just rising to the surface (literally). The weirdness all began during the summer of 1926. One of the benefits of small town living is that the pace of life during the summer months often moves at a glacial speed, leaving plenty of leisure time to soak up the beauty of the local lake. Picture a beautiful August day where the entire town retreats to the refreshing lake water in an effort to escape the summer heat…only to find that they are not the only ones cooling off at the lake. According to the *La Crosse Tribune and Leader Press*, several residents spotted a monster lurking in Humbird Lake. Witnesses generically described the beast as being over four feet long and estimated that it had to

Lake Monsters of Wisconsin

weigh somewhere between 50 and 100 pounds. If witnesses were able to gather a more thorough description of the beast—including it color, shape, and movement, those details were not provided by the newspaper. Instead, the newspaper simply called it a "mysterious animal," and speculated that it might have been "an alligator or some form of sea serpent." One of the hallmarks of small communities is that news tends to travel fast—and strange news travels instantaneously—so you can imagine the amount of curiosity that was generated by just this one sighting. Not looking to let the mystery linger on for too long, the newspaper suggested that perhaps it may prove "necessary to seize the water of the lake," in order to determine the beast's true identify. Despite all the talk, the mysterious animal was never captured.

For years I had simply chalked up this case as a singular anomaly, a one off sighting where something very odd made a brief appearance, disappeared, and in due time, was conveniently forgotten about. For years, this case sat in my "incomplete" file, joined by hundreds of others that were left open due to a lack of information. If what witnesses saw was merely an alligator, being a cold-blooded animal would all but guarantee that it would not survive the harsh Wisconsin winters, thus making a repeat sight-

The calm waters of Emerson Lake

The Elusive Beast of Lake Emerson

A 1939 article touting the mysterious monster

ing extremely unlikely. Yet, on the off chance that the beast was something far more bizarre than a gator, I grasped onto the optimist chance that future sightings might continue. Little did I know that my optimistic attitude would pay dividends. After a 13-year hiatus, the beast of Humbird Lake made a triumphant return, and this time, residents were able to gather a much clearer look.

In 1939, when a female angler decided to spend a beautiful July day out fishing on the lake, she had no idea that her story would soon add to the lake's mysterious history. The unnamed woman's story was captured by the *Madison Capital Times*, which headlined the article "Mysterious Sea Monster is Seen Near Humbird." Although the woman was the first to spot the unknown creature, many others soon flocked to her to also catch a glimpse of the beast. There, sprawled out on the lakeshore was a four-foot-long pea-green creature armed with "deep powerful jaws." Fearful for their safety, several onlookers hurriedly sought out some firearms, but before they had time to return with the arsenal, curiosity overtook the scene, causing one man to smack the beast with a long pole. With the forceful strike the beast "slid back into the lake with a splash of its mighty tail," where it disappeared from sight. Several adrenaline fueled witnesses were convinced that the creature was nothing more than a gator, but the newspaper openly questioned the beast's odd color along with its presence in northern waters. Not everyone was convinced by the alligator theory, as many other eye-witnesses held the view that the beast was "a lizard or a salamander grown to enormous size." The newspaper concluded their story with the following paragraph:

A few years ago a peculiar water creature of large proportions was sighted in the same waters, and as it was never captured nor identified it is possible the present visitor may be the same specimen but now grown larger.

The newspaper did not specify what they meant by "a few years ago." Were they referencing the 1926 (13 years) sighting, or were there other sightings in between that I have yet to discover?

With these two odd sightings in hand, I made my way to Humbird to grab a first-hand look at Emerson Lake. One of the first things that jumped out at me was how shockingly small the lake was. While standing on shore, the 34 acres of the lake make it feel more like an overflowed pond than the home of a giant water beast. When you also figure in that the mean depth of the lake is only 4 feet, it becomes increasingly difficult to fathom that such a large creature could continue to roam undetected in such a limited body of water. On the flipside, the smallness of the lake provides anyone sitting on the boat landing dock an uninterrupted view of nearly the entire lake. While I was scouring the water in search of the beast, I did witness several large fish jumping in the middle of lake. After a few minutes of scanning the lake, I came across a park employee who immediately touted the lake's good fishing conditions. His personal stories of landing some extremely large northern, bass, and catfish at least gave some evidence that the lake is able to sustain large creatures. Setting the diminutiveness of the lake aside, I continue to grasp onto my optimistic hope that sightings of the beast will continue on for many generations.

The Fowler Lake Lop Jaw

Where To Encounter It

Fowler Lake is in Oconomowoc and is located directly south of Lac La Belle Lake.

Creature Lore

Out of the four bunched together lakes (Fowler, Oconomowoc, Lac La Belle, and Okauchee), Fowler Lake has the most documented lake monster stories attached to it. In 1876, a letter written by a Wisconsin resident found its way to the *Chicago Tribune*. The letter provided, in great detail, several of the large "fish" stories of Fowler Lake. The writer told the tale of "old Lop-Jaw," a notoriously elusive fish whose uncanny ability to escape capture was only equaled by its gargantuan size. The prized catch became something of an obsession for a Dr. Henshall, who claimed that

Lake Monsters of Wisconsin

the beast was "as long as an oar." The doctor was lucky enough to actually hook the monster before it easily shook its head and spit out the lure, which shot up twenty feet into the air. Judging by the strength in which the beast tugged on his pole, the doctor believed the beast must have easily weighed over 100 pounds. Distinguishing "old Lop-Jaw" from other fish in the lake was pretty simple due to the fact that it was missing one half of its face, and the other half was pierced with numerous hanging lures. Knowing that its favorite hangouts were down by the dam, Church Point, and the bay at Draper's Hall also increased the chances of finding it.

An 1892 *Chicago Tribune* article touting Wisconsin's lake monsters spent most of its space on the legend of Fowler Lake. In June of 1886, Mr. C.I. Peck was fishing on the lake when "a very large object" caught his notice, and prompted him to steer his boat toward the object. As he inched his way forward, the unknown beast appeared to be a fish and, judging by the portion that was visible, the thing was huge. Peck estimated that the beast was no smaller than eight feet in length and had to weigh upwards of sixty or seventy pounds. If we can believe Mr. Peck's estimates, both the length

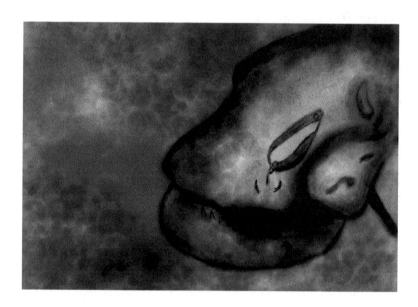

and weight of the beast would be far too great to be attributed to any known fish in the lake.

The lake is home to many paranormal legends

Nearly 20 years later, the mysterious beast had still not yet been caught, assuming that "old Lop-Jaw" was the same creature prowling the lake. In the summer of 1905, Fowler Lake was once again abuzz with talks of a giant fish—this time it was thought to be a huge pickerel. The *Waukesha Freeman* recounted the intriguing story of a Mr. Griffith, who had rigged up a "specially strong spoon" in hopes of landing the new prized fish, which was estimated to be around forty pounds. Luckily, Griffith was able to hook the monster, and furiously fought with it for over a half hour in hopes tiring it out. Finally, another fisherman, Tom Francey, grabbed a net and came to Griffith's aid just as the line snapped, and the fish darted off, with the special lure hanging out of its mouth.

If there was such a thing as the Fowler Lake champion angler award, George Town would have certainly won it. In 1908, Mr. Town was able to catch what the *Waukesha Freeman* claimed was "the largest pickerel ever caught in Fowler Lake." Succeeding where others had failed, the young fishing expert landed a 47-inch pickerel that weighed in at 22.5

pounds. There was no mention as to whether this was the infamous old Lop-Jaw or if the beast had any trophy lures attached to it.

Outside of the giant beast, Fowler Lake has another remarkable connection to the supernatural that comes in the form of the alleged haunted cemetery that rests along the lakeshore. La Belle Cemetery is home to reports of disembodied lights and mysterious noises, but the overwhelming majority of people who visit the cemetery come to see the moving statue. Legend tells of a young woman who went swimming in Fowler Lake, only to tire out, making the lake her watery grave. Eventually her body was buried in a proper grave next to the very lake that took her life. A giant statue stands atop the woman's grave. Legend states that if you visit the woman's grave at night (of course), several anomalies can be witnessed. The statue's hands will turn black right in front of you, and blood will ooze out of its eyes. Yet, the most bizarre legend tells of the statue actually coming to life and recreating the woman's drowning in the lake. Those who have seen her move claim that as soon as the stature descends into Fowler Lake, it instantaneously returns to its grave. Perhaps even the ghostly statue of a drowned woman is frightened by what lurks in Fowler Lake.

The Fox Lake Lurker

Where To Encounter It

The lake is next to the town of Fox Lake. There are several options available to you if you want to get a closer look at Fox Lake including a public boat ramp, several lakeside resorts, restaurants, and saloons.

Creature Lore

The field of paranormal research is chock-full of reports from witnesses who claim to have encountered some type of beast that was seemingly unknown to science. Hikers have come face to face with large Bigfoot creatures, ranchers have seen El Chupacabras devour their cattle, and motorists claim to have spotted giant werewolf beasts roaming the back roads. Yet, for the surprisingly vast array of mysterious sightings, not one body

Lake Monsters of Wisconsin

or carcass of these creatures has ever surfaced, and no living specimen has ever been captured. Looking to explain the lack of any such smoking gun (or in this case body) some researchers have purposed the theory that perhaps these creatures do not permanently reside within our planet, dimension, and/or time. Therefore, based on this theory, the reason we have not captured Bigfoot or discovered the decomposed remains of a hellhound is because they are only momentary visitors here, possessing the ability to come and go at their leisure, leaving behind little physical evidence of their supernatural travels. If such a tantalizing theory were ever proven to be true, it would certainly help explain why the Fox Lake monster was spotted for a brief moment—never to be seen again.

During the summer of 1892, Commodore Clawson and Captain Potts, who operated a steamer on Fox Lake, set off a firestorm of excitement when they reported that a giant monster was dwelling in the depths of the lake.

Captains were ever fearful of the monster

The Fox Lake Lurker

According to the *Milwaukee Journal*, the two men "were going out on a moonlight trip after a picnic party" when their peaceful night was interrupted by the sight of something unusual moving through the water. Just four rods (66 feet) from the side of the boat the men noticed a large beast "with its head and about two feet of its neck sticking out of the water." From what they could see poking out of the water, they estimated the neck and head of the beast to be "about eight or ten inches in diameter." The two stunned men watched the dark slate colored beast take "off at a tremendous speed with its head out of the water." When the beast got about 10 rods away (165 feet) it simply sank down out of sight. The darkness of the night had significantly obscured most of the beast's body, yet judging from "the wake left from the swaying body of the monster the gentleman described it as about twenty feet long."

As one would expect, word of the strange moonlit sightings sparked "great excitement" within the Fox Lake community. Soon curious boaters of all types were patrolling the waters in search of the 20-foot serpent, apparently to no avail as the newspaper article also noted that "no signs of its reappearance have been reported."

Even though the *Waukesha Freeman* claimed that the witnesses "swear positively that they saw the monster as described," the newspaper didn't refrain from suggesting that the curious parties looking for the monster would be better off using a schooner (German beer glass), and if that didn't "fetch him, go on to a double decker." The media of that era took great pleasure in writing off lake monster sightings as nothing more than glassy-eyed ramblings from those who imbibed a little too much liquor. However, I found no mention anywhere suggesting that Commodore Clawson and Captain Potts were anything other than stone cold sober when the monster appeared. Not looking to let the matter rest as the mere delusions of drunkards, the *Waukesha Freeman* cast doubt on the credibility of the sighting by opining that the sighting was a publicity stunt which would most certainly be a fantastic draw for the Fox Lake summer resorts.

Lake Monsters of Wisconsin

Is the Fox Lake monster real or myth?

As I made my way around Fox Lake I talked with many residents about the local lake monster legend and, much to my surprise, a few people expressed familiarity with the odd story. I was told that the story of some unknown monster inhabiting Fox Lake first originated with the American Indians of the area, who were said to believe that something large had once made its home in the lake. It is a very difficult process to ascertain the true meaning behind many American Indian legends. Passed from one generation to another through oral storytelling, many Native legends are multi-layered and smothered in vagueness, and often times these creatures only exist in the spirit realm. Since I have been unable to locate any formal documentation of the alleged Native legends surrounding Fox Lake's serpent, I can only speculate as to whether these stories featured an ancient water spirit (water panther), which is more of a spirit world creature, or if the stories told were that of a more flesh and blood creature that we generally believe to be a genuine sea-serpent.

The Fox Lake Lurker

Outside of luring curious vacationing tourists to Fox Lake, what can we make of this one time sighting? Perhaps it was simply a misidentification spurred on by the trickery of the moonlight. Yet, one would think it would take more than a simple trick of light to fool two seasoned sailors. Maybe the newspaper got it right by deeming it to be nothing more than a publicity stunt meant to put Fox Lake resorts on the map. Unfortunately, the truth of this case may forever evade us as the only real evidence of the creature sank back underwater on that moonlit summer night of 1892.

The Half Moon Monster

Where To Encounter It

Half Moon Lake in Eau Claire provides the intrepid monster hunter with a couple of boat landings, several parks, and even a nice swimming beach to encounter the beast.

Creature Lore

I'm proud to say that Eau Claire is my hometown; I spent the first 30 years of my life exploring all of the various nooks and crannies of the Sawdust City. With Eau Claire as my base of operations, I was able to uncover more paranormal legends there that any other place that I have ever researched. Amazingly, Eau Claire is filled with nearly every type of paranormal and supernatural legend possible. I have investigated numerous

The Half Moon Monster

haunted places including graveyards, bridges, saloons, back roads, and nearly every other conceivable type of location. I have checked out puzzling crop formations that appeared overnight out in the country, deadly mysterious beasts devouring livestock, and mysterious UFOs buzzing through the night. Yet in all my research into the bizarre goings on of the Chippewa Valley, I had never once heard so much as a whisper about a sea serpent. In fact, if it wasn't for a weird twist of chance, I may have never discovered the Half Moon Monster.

My lucky break came while I was researching some old water monster sightings near Oshkosh. I was digging for possible newspaper accounts of the Oshkosh serpent when I stumbled across an article published in the April 20, 1900 edition of the *Eau Claire Leader*. Even though the article was focusing on a strange alligator shot near Oshkosh, it oddly ran the headline "The Half Moon Lake Alligator." The first small paragraph of the article declared that "twelve years ago, people wouldn't believe there was an alligator in Half Moon Lake," before segueing into the Oshkosh alligator story. I quickly did the math, expanded the years in hopes of finding a greater mystery, and began pursuing the Eau Claire newspapers from the 1880s and 90s hoping to discover more about this Eau Claire alligator, even if no one at the time had believed it. After spending several days scouring through the local newspaper archives I discovered that not only did Eau Claire have a sea serpent mystery, but that contrary to the *Eau Claire Leader* article, quite a few people actually believed it to be true.

Everyone in Eau Claire is familiar with Half Moon Lake. Its 135 acres are heavily used by boaters, canoeists, anglers, beach combers, and water sport enthusiasts. Its location right next to the extremely popular Carson Park ensures that constant traffic passes its borders. Up until 2006, the local water skiing team (Ski Sprites) had spent the previous 43 years performing their weekly summer shows on the lake. On any given day you can find an assortment of people fishing along the lake's shores hoping to land a whopper. While not an extremely deep lake (6-foot average, 13-foot maximum), the water's very low clarity makes for the perfect hiding spot for aquatic beasts. As a kid I spent many days playing in the sand of the quaint Half Moon Lake Beach. I can't accurately recall whether or not I actually swam in the lake due to the never ending thick, green, slimly algae sludge which overran the lake each summer. For decades scientists and environmentalists have tried to find solutions to combat the aggressive green algae and would remove tons of the gunk every year, which only spawned untold jokes about the lake being toxic.

As for the mysterious creature, it appears that the Half Moon Monster first appeared during the summer of 1886. It terrorized the locals for a few years, and then simply disappeared into the semi shallow depths of the lake never to be heard from again. Apparently, the creature had done such an excellent job at hiding that within just a couple of decades, the legend of the Half Moon Monster had all but faded into oblivion.

It is ironic that although I stumbled onto this case while digging up stories on Wisconsin alligators, I would soon find out that the alligator was merely one of the many explanations that were being tossed out in hopes of solving this peculiar mystery.

The first printed reference to the Half Moon Monster came in the form of a flippant warning issued by the July 12, 1886 edition of the *Eau Claire Daily Free Press*. The article claimed that "boys who are in the habit of bathing in Half Moon lake are no doubt greatly edified with the curbstone recitals of the vast proportions of a reptile that is said to inhabit its waters." Although no specific size dimensions of the beast were given, we can theorize that the creature was fairly large due to the paper's claim that when the creature surfaced "it gave the saw logs in the vicinity the appearance of straws." After some dull joking banter about the creature looking to dine on unsuspecting swimmers, the paper facetiously claims that "until these 'curdling' accounts of this innominate monstrosity have been exploded, the boys who are inclined to be over credulous will probably go

The Half Moon Monster

The lake during its logging days
(Courtesy of the Chippewa Valley Museum)

elsewhere when they feel that they must sport in the water." Even though this is obviously a tongue-in-cheek reporting job, the article does cast light on the fact that the origin of the legend predates the article, although the length of such pre-dating remains uncertain.

Just two days later, and with a somewhat more serious tone, the *Eau Claire Daily Free Press* published another article on the legend with the headline "There May be Something There." Still obviously skeptical regarding the "current talk of the presence of a foreign monster in Half Moon lake," the paper acknowledges that "there are those who are sincere in the belief that an alligator of some kindred reptile has strayed from his native haunts" and somehow found its way into Half Moon Lake. As I was about to soon find out, not only did Eau Claire have a full-fledged lake monster legend on its hands, it also amazingly had several monster hunters, too. According to the *Eau Claire Daily Free Press*, one "experienced hunter" armed with a rifle had been keeping a diligent eye on the lake "in the hope of catching

Lake Monsters of Wisconsin

a glimpse of the extraordinary game." The most common explanation for the monster was that it had "found its way into the lake through the canal about two weeks ago," (the canal connected the lake with the Chippewa River) a theory that was bolstered by the assertion of two men who claimed to have spotted the giant creature as it moved through the canal.

The Half Moon Monster

The Half Moon Monster

No other specific details of the creature were provided because their sighting occurred during the darkness of evening hours, thus the witnesses could only indistinctly see the beast. Even as the legend continued to grow, the paper firmly believed that when all was said and done the case would surely amount to nothing more than "much cry and little wolf."

On July 17, a rival newspaper, *The Eau Claire News*, looked to pin the Half Moon Lake Monster squarely on the shoulders of the *Eau Claire Leader* newspaper, writing, "There can be no reasonable doubt that the only monster or reptile of an unusual character that ever hung around Half Moon lake has been located in the Leader office."

July 26th must have been slow day at the *Oshkosh Daily Northwestern*, because it included two separate stories about Half Moon Lake within its four-page paper. The first short report tells of an unusually large turtle that had been captured at the lake. At over three feet in length and eighteen inches wide, the turtle certainly could have been responsible for some of the alleged serpent sightings. Three days later, the *Eau Claire Daily Free Press* claimed that residents of the Sixth Ward confirmed the reported dimensions of the giant turtle, although they contend the "animal had to be well drawn out" to reach the hulking size ascribed to it.

The second more interesting story cast even more doubt on the alligator theory by telling the story of Mr. N. Stokes, who, while fishing in Half Moon Lake, "saw a sturgeon of unusual proportions." Stokes claimed that the aquatic beast was "fully six feet in length" and had a monstrous head that constituted about "one-third of the total length of the fish." Lake sturgeon have notoriously been blamed for sea serpent sightings throughout the world, but the alleged offending sturgeon of Half Moon Lake was never captured.

As the summer was winding down, so were the sightings of the mysterious beast. On August 12, the *Burlington Weekly Hawkeye* (Iowa) looked to throw its two cents in on the mystery by claiming that a "sea serpent has wandered into the Chippewa River and is terrorizing the people of Eau Claire." Perhaps the creature was spotted in the Chippewa River, as there were various channels connecting the lake to the river (these channels have since filled in), or maybe the Iowa newspaper simply got the location of the serpent mixed up. Either way, I continue to keep a vigilant eye on the Chippewa River just in case the report was accurate.

During the heart of the summer of 1887, the serpent talk was reignited thanks to a short blurb about the beast in the June 19th edition of the *Daily Leader*. The newspaper reported that the "wandering vagabond" had once again been spotted in Half Moon Lake, leading the newspaper to ask if the beast was a "whale or minnow."

In 1891, the legend of the serpent once again resurfaced through the September 4th edition of the *Chippewa Falls Herald*, which briefly teased about Eau Claire having "a five-legged horse, and hints of a sea serpent in Half Moon lake." As was so frustratingly common during those times, the one sentence "article" provided no further details on either the horse or the serpent.

Following the trend of sea serpents from around the world, sightings of the Half Moon Monster were all but extinguished by the turn of the 20th century. However, even though official reports of the serpent dried up, other aquatic oddities did appear in Eau Claire throughout the years. In 1906, a "monster black snake" was "disturbing the peace of residents on Water Street." The mayhem-causing antics of the snake were reported in the October 4th edition of the *Eau Claire Leader*, which claimed that the beast "must be at least six feet in length." Looking to distinguish this creature from the common everyday snake, the newspaper quoted several eyewitnesses who stated that the beast had a mouth "as wide as a crocodile" and the body the size "of a kangaroo." Even with the newspapers calling this creature a snake, I was immediately struck by the possibility of this beast being the same one that had been spotted in Half Moon Lake. One

The Half Moon Monster

doesn't need to have a splendid imagination to see how a beast with a crocodile's mouth and kangaroo's body might be mistaken for an alligator. The surest way to know would be to capture the beast and put it through more thorough physical examinations. Unfortunately, this capture did not come to fruition. After several fruitless attempts to apprehend the beast, the fate of the "Water Street Monster" was being left to ex-alderman Martin Page, whose experience in woodworking apparently had put him in contact with many types of snakes. Perhaps Page was the same hunter that had tried to lure in the Half Moon Monster, because neither beast was ever captured. During my college days I spent many nights down on Water Street (a typical strip of college bars), and although I witnessed a lot of strange events, I never did lay eyes on the Water Street Monster.

In 1908, local fisherman James Raymond was fishing on the Eau Claire River near the Linen Mill when he made a truly bizarre catch. On the other end of Raymond's pole was a spirited sword fish. Raymond was so perplexed by the out of place fish that he brought it down to the *Eau Claire Leader* newspaper offices, where his catch still showed signs of life. The newspaper listed its dimensions as being "about three feet in length" with a sword "a little more than six inches long." Just how a sword fish, which normally is a salt water specimen, ended up in the fresh waters of the Eau Claire River remained a mystery.

Since discovering this legend, I have brought up the Half Moon Monster to countless historians, librarians, long-time residents, friends and family, and I have yet to encounter one person who is aware of this strange Eau Claire legend. Like so many other fascinating stories of the past, it appears that the Half Moon Monster legend spent the last 120 years being lost to history, which is how I suppose the ever-lurking monster would like it to stay.

Jenny: The Monster of Lake Geneva

Where To Encounter It

Geneva Lake is located in Lake Geneva. Geneva Lake can be accessed directly behind downtown Lake Geneva. The public beach area provides a wonderful viewing area over the lake.

Creature Lore

In the depths of Geneva Lake is a giant scale-covered sea serpent that has been spotted for thousands of years. Described by witnesses as a mammoth snake-like creature, the mysterious monster has been lurking beneath the surface and terrifying visitors to the area for quite some time. Locals say that the creature is some type of dinosaur descendant that was passed over by time and evolution. Over the decades, reports of this un-

Jenny: The Monster of Lake Geneva

derwater dweller have continued to baffle both researchers and tourists alike.

Today Lake Geneva is a bustling resort town overflowing with tourists and seasonal residents. Situated only mere miles from the Illinois border, Lake Geneva flourishes from the steady influx of Chicagoans desperate for a vacation. Yet, long before the area was bombarded by tourists, American Indians took advantage of the area's fertile farming lands and access to the waters of Geneva Lake. It is estimated that tribes were living in Lake Geneva as far back as 1000 B.C. While no recorded evidence of the natives encountering the mysterious creature inhabiting Geneva Lake has yet been discovered, one piece of possible evidence was destroyed during development. Years ago in Lake Geneva sat two effigy mounds that were believed to have been constructed by unknown native hands. While one of the mounds was shaped in the form of a panther, the other posed an even greater mystery, as it was constructed in the shape of a giant serpent or lizard. Was this effigy mound created to record to sightings of a mysterious serpent the tribe had actually encountered, or was it designed for some other purpose? Unfortunately that question will have to remain unanswered due to the fact that years ago, while the area was experiencing expanded growth and development, the effigy mounds were removed, thus relegating their possible secrets to nothing more than speculation.

The first white pioneers visited the area in 1831. Perhaps the white settlers were warned of the sea monster by the indigenous people, because reports of the unknown sea monster quickly followed. Those who live in the area believe that even though much of the native people's presence has all but disappeared, the belief that a sea serpent inhabits the waters of Geneva Lake continues on. In order to shed some light on the legend we must first examine the lake itself, which is Wisconsin's second largest lake. The expansive lake measures three miles wide, nine miles long, and over 150 feet deep. With such sheer size, the lake offers plenty of room for some unknown creature to reside. Today, the local tourism bureau states that on

Lake Monsters of Wisconsin

the bottom of the lake one can find an assortment of odd items including a Volkswagen, a 50's era cabin cruiser, and even the hull of the Lady of the Lake ship. Perhaps with such an established history of mysterious sightings, they can now add the sea serpent to that list.

My first expedition to the area came during the fall, when the area was mostly cleared out of the sunbathing visitors, allowing me to grab a mostly unimpeded view of the lake. The wide lake shore border is composed of both public beach areas and private million-dollar lakefront estates. What makes the legend of the lake's large snake-like serpent especially fascinating is the clearness of the waters where it is said to roam. On a good day, the water provides an excellent unimpeded view many feet down. Like most of my investigations, this case began with the need to dig up some additional research on the legend of the serpent. My first stop was the local library, where several of the librarians were puzzled by the request for information on the lake monster. This is nothing new, as many old legends have nearly been forgotten by most. Fortunately, I was directed to a reference librarian who had collected several articles of past sightings. Armed with a good selection of old newspapers on microfilm, and plenty of equipment, the adventure into the Geneva Lake serpent was about to begin.

It is believed that the legend of the Geneva Lake monster dates back to the American Indians who roamed the land, yet outside of the effigy mounds, no recorded evidence of their sightings has surfaced. Like many other American Indian cultures, the stories were passed down through the oral tradition of storytelling. Local tales tell of the Potawatomi believing that in the depths of the lake dwelled a water monster that was formed in the shape of a giant eel or snake. The original inhabitants of the area proceeded with caution whenever they ventured close to the waters. According to legend, their trepidation around the lake was based on prior experiences when canoes were tipped over and sunk by the deadly serpent. If any member of the tribe suddenly went missing, the serpent was the first to receive blame. However, what the natives lacked in officially

Jenny: The Monster of Lake Geneva

Does Jenny lurk in Geneva Lake?

recording their sightings, the white settlers more than made up for, and so began the modern legend of Geneva Lake's monster that is affectionately known as "Jenny."

While the locals were busy seeing the creature appear all over the lake, the newspapers were equally busy spreading stories of the legend throughout their pages. In 1892, the *Xenia Daily Gazette* briefly touched on the legend, stating that it was an "indescribable monster" that suddenly appeared in Geneva Lake. During the following years it appears as though the creature became very territorial and seemed hell bent on causing trouble for boaters. In his book, *The W-Files*, researcher Jay Rath wrote of several accounts during the 1890s in which unaware boaters would be out enjoying a day on the lake when, out of nowhere, the water would begin to mysteriously boil up around their boat. Within seconds the boaters would find themselves thrown into the waters as some unseen force capsized their boat.

Lake Monsters of Wisconsin

On August 12, 1899, the *Wisconsin State Journal* ran an article that described the lake serpent as being a "thirty-foot monster." With such extraordinary claims coming from all directions, the Geneva Lake monster legend was just getting started.

Even the turn of the century was not enough to slow down the legend, as the early 1900s were especially rife with serpent sightings. In July of 1892, the *Chicago Tribune* covered a magnificent sighting on the banks of the lake. The article tells of Ed Fay, who took two young boys out fishing. The group had spent the day out trolling the lake in hopes of landing a bass or two. As the afternoon wore on the fishermen caught their fill, and the group was about to head back to enjoy their catch when "suddenly there arose out of water within a few rods of the boys the monstrous head of a huge serpent with large, fierce-looking eyes and wide open mouth, in which they could plainly see several rows of sharp, hooked teeth." Amazingly, the creature raised its head a clear 10 feet out of the water and slowly crept toward the boys. Nearly paralyzed with fear, the trio huddled together as they saw the creature's fish-like scales reflect off the glaring sun. As the beast got closer, the boys were able to see that while the underbelly

A drawing of the encounter that appeared in the Chicago Tribune in 1892

Jenny: The Monster of Lake Geneva

of the beast was greenish in color, its back was completely black. With the beast now within feet of the boat, the boys' fear nearly consumed them as they waited for the beast to attack. Yet, almost as though it could sense the fear in the air, the serpent let out a thunderous roar, unexpectedly turned course and darted off for the center of the lake. Still dazed from the whole experience, it took the guys several moments before they got the nerve to retreat to the safety of the shore. Once back on the land, the boys immediately told their experience to other witnesses who were gathered around the shore line. According to the group, the creature was all of 100 feet long and was a staggering 3 feet in diameter at its largest spot. As the boys swore they would not return to the lake, other onlookers reported losing sight of the beast near Kaye's Park. Word of the unbelievable serpent story quickly spread, and within hours the banks of the lake were swarming with hundreds of excited onlookers hoping to catch a glimpse of the magnificent beast of the lake.

A few months later on September 28, 1902, the serpent made another surprise appearance in broad daylight. Mrs. Buckingham was sitting on the porch of her cabin near Reid's Park, when she noticed a strange serpent coiling and roiling not too far from the shoreline. Mrs. Buckingham could not believe her eyes and stated that the creature had to be at least 65 feet in length, with a perfectly round body that expanded nearly 10 inches in diameter. Whatever the creature was, it was moving through the water with an undulating motion that splashed the water and sent out waves in all directions. The commotion quickly attracted a half-dozen other witnesses who reported that only portions of the creature's body could be seen on the surface of the water. In all her life, Mrs. Buckingham had never seen such a monstrosity and called out to her neighbor, Mrs. Dorliska Reid, to alert her of the beast. Mrs. Reid's two young children, along with another boy, came running to the scene. Upon spotting the creature, the brave young men hurriedly grabbed a row boat and gave chase to the serpent with hopes of obtaining a closer look. Perhaps the snake sensed the young men's approach, as it made one last noisy splash before

Lake Monsters of Wisconsin

it quickly disappeared into the depths of the lake. Based on several accounts and varying angles, witnesses confidently placed the length of the water monster to be between 25 and 80 feet. On September 29, 1902, the *Janesville Gazette* ran the following story: "Lake Geneva Sea Serpent." Here the reporter touted the creature as being "sixty-five feet long and from eight to ten inches in diameter." This sighting portrays the serpent as more of a snake-like creature than the traditional sea serpent shape. With multiple sightings occurring every year, the townsfolk dubbed the odd lake inhabitant "Jenny" in honor of their lake.

Eventually the sea serpent craze began to subside. A 1906 *Janesville Daily Gazette* article actively sought out reports of the monster when it asked, "Where are all of the sea serpent and fish stories of the present summer? Both Lake Delavan and Lake Geneva have thus far been free from that awful horror." It seemed like a poignant question, as through the years the number of sighting continued to decrease.

Not all who visited Lake Geneva were firm believers of Jenny's existence. In 1902, the *Lake Geneva Herald* ran an article touting its belief that the serpent was a fake, dreamt up by Chicago journalists in order to sell more newspapers. The article even called into question the sobriety of the "so-called witnesses." More recent skeptics point to the lake's crystal clear waters as evidence disputing the existence of any underwater monster, claiming that any large creature inhabiting the lake would have no place to hide and therefore would have already been caught. However, others believe the bottom-dwelling anomaly rarely surfaces, and when it does, it usually gets spotted by tourists.

Perhaps the most intriguing aspect of the original sightings was the unusual shape of the animal. Instead of having the traditional sea serpent shape complete with humps, Jenny appeared to be more of elongated serpentine-like creature with an unusually lengthy large body. I took great note of this fact as I planned another expedition to Geneva Lake. My sec-

Jenny: The Monster of Lake Geneva

ond expedition to the lake came in the summer of 2010, when the town was at its peak population. While searching the lake for an open space to watch for the serpent, I encountered various reactions from the visitors when I asked about the lake's paranormal history. Unfortunately, many of the newcomers had never heard of the old serpent legends. Over the years, occasional sightings pop up and are discussed by the old timers, but nothing has yet matched the scope and appeal of the early sightings. After several days of scouring the lake, I finally departed without any substantial evidence of the serpent, yet even so, I continue to hope that somewhere out there Jenny is still scaring unsuspecting tourists.

The Lake Delavan Giant

Where to Encounter It

The lake can be accessed through several boat landings, a public beach, a few restaurants, and a couple of lakeside resorts in Lake Delavan.

Creature Lore

Many of the lakes in this book simply would not have the depth to secretly house a 40-foot deadly monster, but with pockets of Delavan Lake reaching depths over 55 feet, the monster could easily stretch out without having to ever break the surface.

Normally, the overall believability of sightings dealing with paranormal phenomena is heavily influenced by the perceived credibility of the main witness. If the witness was known as the stumbling town drunk, the sightings immediately got explained away as simple delusions brought on by the drink. Conversely, a sighting by an upstanding prominent member of the community is almost always given a high level of credence by the general public. With this fact in mind, it's quite puzzling that although the

The Lake Delavan Giant

main Delavan Lake witness was a Sunday school superintendent, much of the media still portrayed him as an intoxicated vagrant.

Like most anglers who set out for a day of fishing, Mr. Otto Schott had high hopes that this time he would land a whopper. Sitting in his boat near Nelson's bar, it would have been nearly impossible for Mr. Schott to have foreseen that instead of reeling in the whopper, he himself was about to become its prey. The entire terrifying experience was detailed in the August 25, 1902 edition of the *Oshkosh Daily Northwestern* which wrote that as Mr. Schott was pulling his boat away from shore he "saw a glowing green light come up out of the water some distance away." At first Mr. Schott paid little attention to the light, believing that it was nothing more than a lantern flashing on the diving pier. His opinion quickly changed when he noticed another identical light appear and "to his horror a great head became distinct, and he saw that the green, glowing lights were the eyes of a fearful creature." What happened next could only be described as fantastical, although many would come to see it as completely delusional. As Schott sat spellbound in his boat, some sort of gigantic body rose up out of the water, and right before his eyes was a hideous 45-foot long reptile whose five-foot wide body was completely covered in huge "yellow scales that shone like brass." The beast was able to contract and elongate these scales "in the manner of a telescope." Schott's attention was quickly drawn back to the creature's eyes, which he described as being set "in a mammoth lion-like head with an enormous toothless mouth." The fact that the beast had no discernable teeth did little to alleviate Schott's fear, especially since the creature was sporting a huge protuberance between its eyes and nose that produced a strange humming noise as the creature moved through the water.

Apparently up until this time the creature was blissfully unaware of Mr. Schott's presence on the lake, but once it laid eyes on the frightened fisherman it "went into such a convulsion of rage, that the water was churned into fury for a quarter of a mile." Still incapable of truly processing what

Lake Monsters of Wisconsin

was transpiring right before his eyes, Schott continued to remain motionless as the beast began to circle its tail around his boat. To his horror, he watched as the beast "took its tail between its jaws and began to contract," evidently looking to crush the boat along with its petrified occupant. Fearing that his life was in imminent danger, Schott somehow garnered the courage to stand up and plunge himself from the boat by quickly diving underneath the creature. When he finally popped up to catch his breath, he "heard a horrid crunching sound, and looking back he saw that where the boat had been" was nothing more than "a great mass of splinters." Swimming as fast as his lungs would allow, Schott frantically sought out the perceived safety of the shore. Once on solid land, he darted toward the hotel, only to collapse from the exhaustion of his escape. Looking like a man fearful of losing his life, Schott's appearance and condition only helped to provide credence to his bizarre story. His death defying escape quickly prompted the cancellation of scheduled yachting parties and even love-struck beachcombers retreated from the shoreline in fear that the deadly beast would be on the prowl for other victims.

The sighting caused such an uproar in the community that for several days and nights the shoreline around the lake was overflowing with curious onlookers hoping to catch a glimpse of the aquatic predator. Armed with looking glasses, the newspaper claimed that one or two of the spectators had actually spotted the eyes of the beast, while a few others saw the lake "lashed to a fury," and nearly everyone on shore swore that they were able to hear "the dreadful humming sound" of the beast. Even though the splintered pieces of the crushed boat eerily washed ashore, the giant beast itself remained elusive.

Once the news of the outrageous sighting spread, newspapers from around the country had a field day, clamoring over each another to see who could make the first predictably dull play of words on Mr. Schott's name. The *Janesville Daily Gazette* wrote that "Schott, who discovered the sea serpent at Lake Delavan, is properly named." The *Marshall Daily News* out

The Lake Delavan Giant

The creature was spotted by several fishermen

of Michigan made the worst joke, wondering if Mr. Schott's full name was "Mr. Half Schott or, maybe Mr. Seven-fifths Schott." While the *Madison Journal* reported, "Just what brand is most popular at Delavan Lake isn't stated, but with the size of the sea serpent with radiating emerald eyes, reported, suggests wild whiskey rather than the Milwaukee beverage." The *Green Bay Gazette* wrote "The man at Delavan Lake who saw a 40-foot sea serpent had evidently been using marine glasses-schooners." (Schooner of course being a German beer glass). In all the hoopla surrounding the sightings, the fact that Mr. Schott was a superintendent of a Sunday school was either forgotten or intentionally overlooked in order to fit the media's own narrative.

A few days later, in its August 25 edition, the *Racine Daily Journal* claimed that a Mr. Charles Sage, the proprietor of the Highland at Delavan Lake, was visiting town on business and was busy telling any reporter that would listen that since the sea serpent sighting made the newspapers, business at his resort was better than ever before. Apparently not wanting to continue to rake in record profits, Mr. Sage told the newspaper that the "whole thing was a fake, pure and simple." Just what evidence he provided for this statement was not given. Between the drinking humor and the alleged hoax allegation, it would seem that Mr. Schott's sighting would quickly be debunked and forgotten about. Well, as it turns out Schott was by no means the first person to see the monster of the lake.

The same *Oshkosh Daily Northwestern* article that so vividly recounted Mr. Schott's sighting also mentioned other similar monster sightings in Delavan Lake that predated 1902. In fact, the newspaper claimed that Schott's sighting was merely a "reappearance of the monster serpent seen off Nelson's bar a few years ago." Not only had Mr. Schott seen a serpent in the same exact location as others had, but his description of the beast turned out to be "identical with that given by the men who saw it some years ago." As hard as I tried, I was unsuccessful in my quest to uncover any further details regarding the previous sightings. It is quite possible that the past sightings were only talked about as local legend and may have never made it to the pages of a local newspaper.

Many were skeptical that such a giant could exist in the lake

The Lake Delavan Giant

One year later, in 1903, three gentlemen from Janesville found themselves in the same figurative boat as Mr. Schott, for they too saw something big traversing the waters of Delavan Lake. The odd encounter was fully documented in the August 3rd edition of the *Janesville Daily Gazette*. While at a camp on Delevan Lake, the men observed "the head of some large animal or fish protruding some two feet from the water" as it moved in an "unexplainable fashion" through the water. With a neck that was "at least twelve inches in circumference" and a head described only as "simply enormous," if this thing was truly a fish, it was like no fish they had ever laid eyes on. Although the sighting of the beast was fleeting, the discussion as to its true identity continued for many days. Some believed that it was just a big pickerel fish haunting the lake, but Nev. Washburn, who the newspaper dubbed as "an authority on such matters," believed that witnesses were seeing a "deep sea porpoise which he brought from the Gulf of Mexico." The only drawback to the article was that no one had publically come forward to claim ownership of the sightings, and each person the newspaper interviewed claimed ignorance and tried to pass the sightings off onto other people.

In what has become an all too familiar tale, I was unable to locate any additional stories of monsters dwelling in Delavan Lake. However, tales of the beast must have dried up by 1906, because an article in the August 3rd edition of the *Janesville Daily Gazette* openly asked "where are all the sea serpent and fish stories of the present summer. Both Lake Delavan and Lake Geneva have thus been free from that awful horror." In the future I can only hope that the "awful terror" will once again be seen hunting for human prey in Delavan Lake.

The Lake Hallie Whopper

Where To Encounter It

Lake Hallie (Badger Mills) is a small lake just north of Eau Claire in the small town of the same name. Although all of the lakeside resorts are long gone, a public boat launch, boat landing, and small park still exist to search for the monster.

Creature Lore

In the late 1800s, Lake Hallie (also called Badger Mills due to the giant mill located on the lake) was a prime vacation destination tucked between the cities of Eau Claire and Chippewa Falls. Anglers flocked to the waterside resorts, lured in by the lake's reputation as being overflowing with fish. On any given day the lake would be filled with swimmers, boaters, and anglers, so it should come as no surprise that a gigantic out-of-place fish would not remain undetected for long.

The Lake Hallie Whopper

> **BIG FISH IN BADGER LAKE.**
>
> **A Monster Has Been Seen There Several Times Recently.**

An 1885 newspaper article headline touting the monster sightings

In early July of 1895, two young boys were getting their boat ready for a day of fun and fishing when something big near the swimming beach caught their attention. Through the clear water the boys saw the colossus fish resting in about four feet of water. One of the youngsters told the *Eau Claire Free Press* newspaper that the beast was "laying still...just waving his fins and tail a little as if he was asleep." With adolescent curiosity in full bloom, one of the boys quickly poked the creature with an oar, causing the beast to whirl around, using its large tail to foam up the water and make a huge splash, before darting off out of sight. Admitting that he was only able to observe the creature for a short time, one of the boys could only describe it as being a "whopper."

Three weeks later, the beast made another grand appearance. This time the whopper was spotted by a "reliable fisherman" who, while standing on the bank of the lake, noticed the out-of-place fish once again swimming in shallow water. Getting a good look at the beast, the fisherman described it as being "five or six feet long," as it appeared to be trying to get ashore or escape the confines of the lake. The beast was so close to the man that its back stuck right out of the water, prompting the rubber booted fisherman to dash into the lake in a valiant attempt to capture the beast. Not surprisingly, the beast was much too speedy for the fisherman and easily avoided capture while making a "splash like a man falling overboard."

After studying these two sightings you could quickly come to the conclusion that the whopper was merely a very large fish...exciting, but certainly not unknown. An extremely large lake sturgeon, Muskie, catfish, or northern pike could all be large enough to be misconstrued as a monster. In fact, the leading belief among those in Badger Mills at the time was that the beast was indeed a sturgeon. Yet, the challenging problem with this theory is that the relatively small lake had no known species of sturgeon. In addition, one would think that if the beast was a sturgeon, the above-mentioned "reliable fisherman" would have noticed and mentioned it… he did not. One interesting theory was that the creature could have made its way into the lake from the nearby Chippewa River as the lake did connect to the Chippewa River. But the small brook pathway was so shallow that the newspaper claimed there was "no probability that any fish ever came up to the lake from the river." So the question then became, "How did a sturgeon make its way into Lake Hallie?" For the answer, the newspaper blamed Mother Nature. Turning to a more unique and obscure explanation, the newspaper speculated that a small sturgeon "was sucked up in a water spout by cyclonic action from one of the great lakes and deposited where it is now by the clouds." Predating the great supernatural investigator Charles Fort by many years, the newspaper went on opine

The site of the former Badger Mills

The Lake Hallie Whopper

that there were other well-documented cases of fish and minnows raining from the sky. Cases, which it said "lend great plausibility of the theory."

Needless to say, the sightings of the unknown fish caused great excitement with the resort community as evidenced by the newspaper reporting that "the cottagers at the lake are determined to capture the monster and are trolling for him daily with heavy tackle." Since the creature was never caught, nor was its carcass ever washed ashore, the mystery of its true nature may never be known. But that hasn't stopped hopeful people from trying. To this day, Lake Hallie remains a popular destination for hardcore anglers, and perhaps one day some lucky person will hook onto a mystery-solving monster.

The Lake Michigan Leviathan

Where To Encounter It

Lake Michigan runs along the entire east coast of Wisconsin from the northern tip of Door County to the southern shores of Kenosha. There are countless places along the coast for you to get close to the lake—and the monster.

Creature Lore

When it comes to sheer numbers, Lake Michigan sits atop the list of Wisconsin lake monster sightings. It should come as no surprise that such a gargantuan body of water would produce so many unexplained sightings. For the sake of space, I have chosen some of the most interesting and baffling cases from throughout the history of the legend.

Reports of the beast in the water date back to the early days of shipping when sea captains fearfully wrote of 150-foot leviathan beasts that would wrap their dozen or so tentacles around a ship and drag it to the bottom of the lake…never to be heard from again. These encounters were so fantas-

The Lake Michigan Leviathan

SAILOR SEES SEA SERPENT
Mysterious Leviathan of the Deep Pays a Visit to Local Waters.

Newspaper articles detailing sightings by sailors were common in the early 1900s

tical that with today's science we look back on them as being nothing more than highly embellished folktales from inebriated crewmen who had been out to sea for far too long. Yet, the long list of Lake Michigan sightings may just prove that the stories were more fact than fiction.

A brief article in the *Boston Post* tells of an 1883 sea serpent sighting near Sturgeon Bay, leaving townsfolk wondering "why the familiar attraction of summer resorts should be discovered so far inland." On the heels (or fins) of the Sturgeon Bay sighting was the appearance of another creature seen three weeks later near the town of Jacksonport. The *Manitowoc Lake Shore Times* claimed that a "goodly number of respectable and truthful citizens" spotted a "wonderful giant sea serpent." Apparently stuck on a reef, the beast was "lashing the water to foam with its enormous tail, while it raised its horrible head high into the air." One witness, Dr. Al. Chandler, noticed what appeared to be several "young sea serpents" surrounding the big beast as though they were waiting for it to free itself. Finally, with one last gigantic effort, the serpent freed itself from the reef and swam back into the lake, closely followed by those alleged offspring. Once the creature was gone, a party of gentleman took a boat out to the site and noticed the surrounding water was discolored with blood. Closer inspection of the reef reviewed several scraps of skin "which had been torn from the serpent by the rugged rocks." The recovered skin was quickly put on display in town—although the location of the sea serpent display was not given.

Lake Monsters of Wisconsin

After a heavy October rainstorm in 1887, two Racine sisters living on a high bluff near the southern limits of the city caught a glimpse of something odd in the water. At first, the ladies believed they were merely watching a "peculiarly shaped tree" floating in the lake, until the supposed tree "began to move with an undulating motion." It was then that the women noticed another creature of similar size and shape swimming along next to the first one. Unlike so many other non-descript sightings, the *Weekly Wisconsin* wrote that the beasts were both "at least twelve or fourteen or more feet long, and appeared to be as large around as a man's body." Their "heads were large and flat, shaped like a snake's." As one beast took the lead, the other followed behind at a distance of three waves. What struck the women as being odd (outside of seeing a sea monster) was the manner in which the creatures moved. The sisters reported that the beasts swam toward the middle of the lake, but "did not seem to make very rapid progress." Instead they swam with a "slow and steady motion." Several times the creatures appeared to stop, as though they needed a rest in order to continue their trek. As the creatures passed through the waves, they "raised their heads high to keep them above the crests." Remarkably, the ladies watched the strange creature procession for quite some time before the creatures swam out of sight.

Monster hunting was all the rage in the early 20th century, as evidenced by a strange sighting that occurred in 1900. A group of men working for Reichert Construction, near the village of Wind Point, were down by the water collecting sand with several teams of horses and wagons. The men, as reported by the *Racine Daily Journal*, noticed an "immense fish" in the shallow water near shore. The beast was as long as the wagon and horses combined and was "flapping and churning the water at a fearful rate," while spraying a huge volume of water several feet into the air. Frightened by the beast's immense size and demonstrated strength, the workers quickly armed themselves with pickaxes and clubs and charged toward the water. They were looking to smash the beast into submission, but unfortunately the monster easily eluded them by retreating into deep water.

The Lake Michigan Leviathan

The seemingly endless water of the lake

Expanding on the strange sighting, one of the witnesses believed the unknown fish was well over 30-feet in length. This wasn't the only time the leviathan was seen lurking in the shallows. The newspaper also makes reference to several sightings during the previous few years where the monster had also been seen prowling near shore. On those occasions, tug boats had been launched in an attempt to capture the monster, but they, too, returned empty handed.

One of the most bizarre and captivating leviathan sightings occurred in 1903, while several young men were enjoying a day of leisure boating out on the lake. The men were on the opposite side of Racine College when a giant snake-like creature appeared. The snake was 14 feet long, but its 12-inch diameter put its size beyond any snake they had ever seen. Additional details provided by the witnesses squarely maneuvered this sighting to the realm of being downright bizarre. According to the *Racine Journal*, the witnesses were able to see a series of wings, like those of flying fish, all along the beast's body. The sighting became even more perplexing when the monster was said to possess a head like that of an elephant, complete with large horns. Their description was so outlandish that the newspaper

Lake Monsters of Wisconsin

openly questioned whether they were "intoxicated with the lake breezes—or something else." Over the past couple decades, I have learned that we cannot simply dismiss a case because it is too unbelievable, or that it doesn't easily slide into any known category of sightings. Our suspension of disbelief seems to have firmly placed boundaries; we can believe in the possibility of a giant aquatic monster…but only one without wings or horns. Would we place any credibility in sightings of a bright pink Bigfoot, or a UFO made of cotton candy? Yet, when you are dealing with the odd and unusual, what constitutes something as being too odd? Perhaps the aforementioned young men simply reported what they actually saw, no matter how screwy and irrational it sounded. The young men had no idea that their outlandish story of a horned monster would be corroborated in 1910.

An old soldier was willing to "wager his head" that what he saw near Racine in 1905 was indeed some sort of leviathan. The unnamed witness told the *Racine Daily Journal* that he had spotted the "sea serpent" down at the lake, but no further details were provided.

While the horned monster sighting of 1903 was widely ridiculed as being the fanciful dreams of drunken college kids, the odd looking monster made a triumphant return in 1910. This time the monster was seen near the township of Mosel. It was first spotted by Henry Beuchel, who stumbled upon the beast as it was busy sunning itself on shore. Beuchel must have startled the giant, because it quickly splashed back into the water and swam east. It would seem that the creature really enjoyed the warmth of the sun, as later that same day another farmer, Albert Albrecht, saw the beast once again lazily sunning itself on shore. Much like the previous encounter, when Albrecht approached, the monster quickly slipped into the water. The *Sheboygan Daily Press* reported on the strange appearance of the creature as both witnesses believed that the monster was upwards of 25 feet long. It had a "greenish colored head about two feet in diameter." Much like the 1903 sighting, "several horn-like protuberances" adorned its head in all directions, and "two short tusks" hung down from its mouth.

The Lake Michigan Leviathan

Many wrote off the creature as being a sea lion or walrus—an escapee from a local circus or the Chicago zoo. Yet, if the creature did indeed match the witnesses' descriptions, there would be too many discrepancies for it to be a walrus or sea lion. First, neither the walrus nor the sea lion come anywhere near the 25-foot length of the beast. Even a gross witness overestimation of the beast would not make up the difference, as most walruses range between 9-12 feet in length. And while the "two short tusks" definitely fit the physical characteristics of a walrus, we still have no explanation to account for the multiple horns protruding from its head. These points were first explored by Rev. Denninger who also noted to the newspaper that the creature was seen to have a snake-like body—long and sleek—which would put it at odds with the stocky roundish makeup of a sea lion.

Many additional details of the legend were told of in a 1935 *Racine Journal Times* article with the headline "Lake Monster Tale Punctured." The writer shed some light on the history of the creature, claiming that over the years the beast took on various names ranging from "Oscar, Sadie, and Aunt Samantha." During the early 1900s, numerous sightings suggested that the beast was "swallowing fishing nets, pushing tugs around and tunneling a 'cave of death' under the breakwater." The "puncturing" of the legend came from Harold Keyes, who not only claimed that the beast was actually a sea lion, but that he had taken photographic evidence of said sea lion basking in the lake (no photo accompanied the article). Keyes had snuck up on the beast as it basked in the sun, allowing him to positively identify the creature as a sea lion. The newspaper triumphantly declared that Racine "beach-goers now can paddle in the waves without fearing that little Agnes will be grabbed by the hair and wrenched away to a watery lair."

It appears that not everyone was fully invested in the sea lion theory, as one year later the *Sheboygan Press* suggested that the real cause of the monster could be blamed on a school of carp. In the summer of 1936, the

Lake Monsters of Wisconsin

town of Cedar Grove was abuzz with a rash of recent sea serpent sightings in the lake. Witnesses reported seeing some 18-foot creature swimming just eight feet from the shore. Boaters were quickly organized, and when they approached the location of the sighting the alleged sea monster was nowhere to be found. Using the fuzzy logic that since no serpent was captured, the newspaper claimed that it must have been "a school of carp swimming near the top of the water near the shore."

We must keep in mind that these are only the Wisconsin based sightings of the leviathan. The newspaper archives are littered with countless sightings of the beast spotted from the Michigan side of the lake as well. The lake affords the leviathan nearly limitless space to make its way from one state to another, preventing either one from claiming sole ownership of such a wonderful legend.

The Lake Monona Sea Serpent

Where To Encounter It

Lake Monona is not too far from the Capitol Building in Madison, just southeast of Lake Mendota as you cross over Highway 151. The lake can be accessed in numerous spots, including Olin and Olbrich Parks, along with many trails.

Creature Lore

Not everyone was caught up in the sea serpent fever of the late 1800s and early 1900s. Skeptics claimed that these so-called monsters were nothing more than regular fish that were being misidentified. Skeptics rolled out a number of possible fish that, on any given day, could have been mistaken

Lake Monsters of Wisconsin

for a giant marine monster. The most commonly-blamed fish were the Sturgeon, Oarfish, Muskie, and Northern Pike. Some even thought large turtles were at the heart of serpent sightings. However, what seems to expose this theory was the absolute certainty with which the witnesses believed that whatever they had seen was not merely some normal animal. Adamant in their convictions, the witnesses believed that something unknown really did/does lurk in Lake Monona.

In the 1860s, the city of Madison aspired to expand from the Capitol City into a major regional hub of trade, commerce, and tourism. Lakeside hotels and resorts started springing up to entice weary travelers and vacationing families. The ongoing development around Lake Monona spurred some of the first recorded sea serpent reports as the influx of new visitors utilized all portions of the lake. Each summer, as the tourist season grew, so did the reported sea serpent sightings. A credible sighting of a lake monster generated a lot of positive publicity, which in turn drew more tourists, who of course saw more serpents. The whole cycle fed on itself for many years until the reports started to dwindle, and the sea serpent seemed lost to history. As evidenced by the rash of serpent sightings in nearby Lake Mendota, 1892 was a good year for Madison monster hunters, and Lake Monona would not disappoint. "Madison's Lake Snake is Twenty Feet Long," read the June 11, 1892 *Janesville Gazette* article. Norman Morgan was out fishing when he spotted what appeared to be a soaked log lying in the water. "As he sat there looking at the thing he saw one end of it rising out of the water a bit." Bravely, Morgan stood up in his boat and put one of his feet over the side and let it rest on the "log." Just as soon as his foot touched down, Morgan saw that the log was actually a serpent as "large as a telephone pole," with a mouth as large as a barrel. The creature dashed backwards, showing a mouth so big that Morgan claimed, "You could have run a wheel barrel into it." The beast was widely splashing around as though it was trying to get into the boat. In fact, the beast's tail had whipped up so much water that Morgan "was afraid the boat would go down." At a time when most people would have

The Lake Monona Sea Serpent

high-tailed it out of there, Morgan grabbed a big hunting knife and went after the creature, stabbing the serpent an estimated forty times. Unfortunately, this is where the article inexplicably ends, leaving us to ponder what happened next and the ultimate fate of the serpent.

There was also a rash of similar sightings that got much less publicity.

On July 21 Darwin Boehmer and a friend spotted the creature while out on a boat ride. In his book, *The W-Files*, Jay Rath, writes that Boehmer saw the creature moving along the south shore at a good pace. The creature got within 75 feet—so close, in fact, that the men could see that the beast was "undulating in an up-and-down motion. Its head, they said, resembled that of a dogfish." Several others had witnessed the beast from the shore and estimated that it was approximately 10 -15 feet long. A few days later, on July 25, the *Oshkosh Daily Northwestern* wrote that the creature was "heading for the campgrounds of the Monona Lake assembly when seen." Jay Rath wrote of another bizarre 1892 sighting. It was October 7 when an anonymous man rented a boat from John Schott (who also had seen the beast). The man was rowing about and having a good time, when all of a sudden a 20-foot-long monster passed underneath his boat. The man panicked because he believed the creature was attempting

Many swimmers encountered the beast

Lake Monsters of Wisconsin

to capsize the boat and quickly rowed back to the safety of the shore. He vowed never to return to the lake without some handy weapons.

Over the next few years other similar sightings took place, but they received a lot less publicity. On August 24, 1894, the *Janesville Daily Gazette* simply wrote, "Madison's sea serpent has been resurrected."

On June 11, 1897, Lake Monona was again abuzz with news of a spectacular encounter with a sea serpent. The whole episode began when a crowd of onlookers noticed a 20-foot beast traveling along the surface of the lake. The next day the *Wisconsin State Journal* ran the article "What-Is-It-In The Lake?" and wrote that the beast "traveled east on the surface of the lake until Eugene Heath, agent of the Gaar-Scott company, fired two shots into it, when it turned and came back." What happened next is unsure because "either the snake or the spectators appeared to have disappeared." The Journal interviewed Mr. Schott, an eye witness, who

Several locations around the lake serve as monster hotspots

The Lake Monona Sea Serpent

claimed that "its appearance is not that of a serpent...and that its shape was like the bottom of boat, but it was about twice as long." The article goes on to state that Mr. Schott's two sons also caught a glimpse of the beast and "were so firmly convinced that it was a dangerous animal that when two ladies desired to be rowed over to Lakeside neither of the Schotts, who had spent a large part of their lives on the lake, would venture out." Even more amazingly, the paper claimed that the serpent was "probably the same animal which is credited with having swallowed a dog which was swimming in the lake a few days ago." All of the witnesses insisted that what they saw was real and not a joke or some figment of their imagination. The Wisconsin State Journal wrote, "In these years a curious monster, perhaps the same sea serpent, was also observed off the Tonywatha and Winnequah resort shore, on the east side of the lake, by different persons."

So, what happened to all of Madison's sea serpents? One theory claims that they may have all died out, pointing to a story that tells of construction workers dredging off of the Olbrich Park shore when a heavy sand pump pipe became clogged. Workers went to inspect the situation and found several huge vertebrae trapped in the machine. It was believed that these vertebrae were the remains of a deceased sea serpent. Others believe that water demons still reside in the lake and make themselves known to any legend-tripper willing to put in the necessary time.

The Lake Ripley Fright

Where To Encounter It

Lake Ripley is located in Cambridge, WI. Much of the lake is surrounded with private resorts, family cabins and summer homes. However, there are several public access points including the wonderful Ripley Park..For those of you looking to experience the serpent in style, you also have the option of staying at the Lake Ripley Lodge B&B, which is located right on the lake.

Creature Lore

The creature inhabiting Lake Ripley is a bit difficult to classify due to the varying accounts of its shape and size. On one hand, there are plenty of witnesses who have spotted a long snake or worm-like creature in the lake. On the other hand, are the witnesses who have caught glimpses of some-

The Lake Ripley Fright

thing that resembled more of the traditional serpent-like shape (think Loch Ness Monster). Maybe people were seeing several different creatures. It may seem far-fetched, but perhaps if/when the Red Cedar Lake monster moved to Lake Ripley, there was already something else there.

By nearly all accounts, the serpent activity on Lake Ripley began in the summer of 1891. It was thought to be caused by the diminishing water depths of nearby Red Cedar Lake. Locals theorized that the creature that had been spotted so often in Red Cedar Lake had traveled to the deeper Lake Ripley through an underground water channel that was thought to connect the two lakes.

Confusing the timeline a bit is a 1945 article from the *Wisconsin State Journal* that contends that the first sighting of the Lake Ripley monster occurred not in 1891, but in 1861. It tells of two witnesses, Newton Hart and Norman Porter, who were out fishing near the lake's island. The men noticed a "giant animal or fish" come out of the waves. "The serpent had a head the size of a horse's," and was shaped like that of a rattlesnake. The two men stated that the beast went wild—lashing its tail while water sprayed from it nostrils. The creature was estimated to be at least four rods (66 feet) long. However, it is my opinion that the 1945 article simply got the date 1861 confused with 1891. I based this opinion on several pieces of evidence. First, I was unable to find any other accounts of a serpent in Lake Ripley or Red Cedar Lake that pre-dates the 1880s. I also discovered that in 1946, Norman Porter celebrated his Golden Anniversary (50 years) with his wife. If we go by the 1861 date, even if Porter was 15 years old when he witnessed the creature (even though the article did not list him as young man or youngster) it would mean that he was 100 at the time of his anniversary. It would also mean he didn't marry until he was 50 years old—all of which doesn't seem to fit the time period. It is much more plausible that the 1945 article simply got the dates mixed up.

In the September of 1891, the *Janesville Gazette* wrote that because of the lowering water levels in nearby Red Cedar Lake, "grave fears are en-

Lake Monsters of Wisconsin

Plenty of food options for a creature inhabiting this lake

tertained that the serpent is about to change its habitation to Lake Ripley." Indeed, many residents along the shore were positive that they had caught a glimpse of "his snakeship." Within a few short years, word of the serpent had spread far and wide. An 1895 blurb in the *Waukesha Freeman* touted a new summer resort that was opening "at Lake Ripley, of sea serpent notoriety."

Although no actual human deaths had been attributed to the beast, it was responsible for quite a number of close calls. In 1895, three women were enjoying a quiet September walk along the banks of the lake near dusk. According to the *Chicago Daily Tribune*, "A terrible commotion was seen in the water." Whatever was causing the commotion, it was a bit too close to shore for the ladies' comfort. Even though the creature had never attacked a human, it was now well within striking range and the women were on edge. The group cautiously watched as the commotion got larger and larger until the "women were frightened almost into spasms."

The Lake Ripley Fright

Like so many communities of the 1800s, the townsfolk depended on the frozen lake to provide the town's year-round ice supply. Every winter ice harvesters gathered on the ice to begin cutting. The *Chicago Daily Tribune* wrote of an interesting winter encounter that got under the nerves of the even the most hardened ice harvester. In 1895, the men were out near the center of the lake inspecting the thickness and quality of the ice, when they "noticed a peculiar wavy black crease, like a mud stain, beneath the surface of the clear ice." Curious, the men followed the brown line for nearly 100 feet. Then "all at once the black seam began to writhe…and although the ice was a foot thick, it began to crack" and sounded like an ice-gorge breaking in a rapid river. Within seconds, the black line disappeared as quickly as it had appeared. The men were so frightened by this mysterious black line that the paper wrote, "Needless to add, the ice-harvesting was done near the shore for the rest of the season." Even near the safety of the shore, the men were a bit tense as they continued to feel strange motions in the water throughout the winter.

The summer of 1896 did not bring any relief to the sightings…in fact, it was a bumper year for the serpent. Luckily for us, the —documented many of the events. To provide some recreation for their guests, several resorts placed floating platforms in the water. These diving floats were anchored in fifteen feet of water and soon became known as the "monster's playthings." During one July evening just as the sun was setting, one of the floats in front of a hotel suddenly began to rise up into the air. The water around the float was thrashing as many spectators along the shore stated they saw "something like an elephant rise up with the float on its head

Lake Monsters of Wisconsin

like a bonnet." Amazingly, witnesses claimed the float was lifted a clean twenty feet out of the water before it "suddenly dropped with a splash which broke a strong chain used for mooring." Later in the same week, the area was expecting a strong storm to come in. One evening before a storm came in, "a strange rushing noise was heard upon the water." The rushing sound was accompanied by a loud hissing noise like "a cyclone." At that very moment, "something passed over the surface," and witnesses swore it was the giant serpent.

At least one of the local farmers refused to buy into the serpent story. According to the *Chicago Daily Tribune*, "Sheep are being snatched from folds at night on neighboring hillsides." One particular farmer who had lost several of his sheep blamed the killings on dogs. Apparently the farmer would carry a gun with him everywhere, threatening to shoot all the dogs he could find, even though no dogs were ever seen attacking the livestock. Of course, the paper also mentioned how impossible it would be for a dog to be able to swallow a sheep whole.

After so many sightings of the beast, excursion parties were formed to hunt the serpent, and tourists flocked to the shores in hopes of catching sight of the lake monster.

In 1896, the *Osseo-Eleva Journal* ran an article claiming the Lake Ripley sea serpent was nothing more than a hoax brought upon by a local farmer who believed that stories of a serpent would drive away tourists. Apparently, the farmer was fed up with tourists stomping through his meadows and fields in order to get close to the lake. It is alleged that he made up the story of the beast taking away his livestock to ward off potential visitors. Unfortunately, the plan backfired. Droves of tourists clamored for the chance to vacation on lake with a genuine sea serpent, much "to the poor German's disgust." Articles like these were very common and often popped up after years of sightings. My main concern with this article is fact that during this time period, sea serpent sightings caused quite a stir

The Lake Ripley Fright

and garnered a ton of publicity, which almost always resulted in a marked increase in tourists. It seems highly unlikely that any farmer would believe that a serpent story would actually keep visitors away. I am much more willing to entertain the notion that these stories were created in order to increase tourism, not to discourage it. I know that several researchers and authors have written about how panicked the people of Lake Ripley were and how that chaos resulted in the widespread closing of cabins and resorts along the lake. Yet, according to all of the newspaper accounts of the day, the exact opposite was true, as record crowds who were caught up in the serpent frenzy descended upon the lake.

Unlike many of the other lakes in Wisconsin, Lake Ripley's sightings continued well into the 1940s. On July 19, 1945, the *Janesville Gazette* wrote about the resurgence of serpent sightings in the lake. The paper told that many unusual happenings and sounds were being reported by the residents living along the lake. Among these strange happenings was that "a large number of carp had been found in the weeds on the south shore of the lake with huge gashes in their sides." Old-timers also complained that the number of fish in the lake had significantly decreased, the blame being placed in the hungry serpent.

Lake Waubesa's What's It

Where To Encounter It

Lake Waubesa is located near McFarland. The lake can be accessed through several boat landing and public parks.

Creature Lore

Nearly everything we know about the Lake Waubesa serpent sightings comes from the father of Wisconsin serpent folklore, Charles E. Brown. In 1942, Brown completed a small 10-page monograph with the nearly equally long title of *Sea serpents; Wisconsin occurrences of these weird water monsters in the Four lakes, Rock, Red Cedar, Koshkonong, Geneva, Elkhart, Michigan, and other lakes.* This foundational work was published by the Wisconsin Folklore Society and has since been cited by nearly every researcher with an interest in sea serpents. You may have noticed Brown's name extensively referenced throughout this entire guide as well.

Often times serpent stories would come from out of state tourists and vacationers who were jolted out of their relaxation by the sight of these deadly serpents. Such is the tale of an Edwards Park, Illinois, man who rowed his boat out one day to try his luck at fishing while vacationing on the east shore of the lake. The man had just dropped the anchor and took a moment to enjoy the beauty of the placid lake. It was a beautiful day and the calm water provided an excellent view of the lake. As the man gazed out a few hundred yards from his boat, the quiet waters began "to heave and move in swells." Soon a gargantuan body rose up out of the water and revealed its gigantic head. The perplexed fisherman watched intently as he tried to figure out what kind of "giant eel or fish" it might be, and after a few tense moments he decided that it might be in his best interest to pull anchor and retreat back to the safety of the shore. Once on the assumed safety of dry land he immediately began share his odd tale with a throng of curious parties, but his insistence that the dark green beast he saw was 60 to 70 feet long did little to secure his credibility among those who listened. Certainly the quart of "forty rod" (strong whiskey) found in his boat did even less to convince his already skeptical audience. Inebriated or not, he wouldn't be the only one to encounter the beast.

The most interesting account given by Brown tells of one such tale involving a pleasant vacation run amok. The story begins with a husband and wife who were out on a leisurely swim out in front of their summer home near Waubesa Beach. The frolicking couple "were nearly frightened to death" when some large unknown creature suddenly rose up out of the water just a few feet away from them. With glistening eyes, the creature made a deadly approach toward to the terrified couple who wasted no time in exiting the lake as fast as humanly possible. Apparently, the only disagreement the couple had over the details of the sighting came from the argument as to which one of them had reached their cottage door quickest.

Brown also wrote that over the next year or so, several other sightings of the lake monster had been reported, but he deemed that most were "fragmentary and are regarded as more or less unreliable." Since Brown did not cite the origin of the reports—something he did throughout his writ-

Lake Monsters of Wisconsin

ings—we can safely assume that he either came by the stories through the witnesses themselves or perhaps he just picked them up through local legends. Whatever means Brown used to capture the stories, he was two steps ahead of me. I scoured through countless newspaper archives looking for any indication of the monster, and I struck out. I contacted several local historians and historical societies, and I struck out. I personally interviewed numerous residents around the lake hoping to dredge up any long told rumors of serpents, and I struck…well you get the point.

What is perplexing to me is the sheer swiftness in which legends can both originate and disappear. While the rare instance of a legend carrying on for hundreds of years does exist, it is far more prevalent for legends to simply slowly diminish over the years until they finally drift off into obscurity. Charles Brown did his best to keep the legend of Lake Waubesa alive, but unless new sightings rejuvenate interest in the beast, the day may come when no living soul recalls the days of a deadly monster lurking in the lake. To me, a future without these legends is much scarier than any monster I have ever researched.

A view of the lake-circa 1927

The Lake Winnebago Water Beast

Where To Encounter It

Lake Winnebago is near Oshkosh, WI. The lake has 20 public boat landings, 13 public parks, and 1 beach (High Cliff State Park) and all of them nicely supply the perfect spot for those looking to partake in some serpent watching.

Creature Lore

Skeptics often claim that most lakes simply do not provide the sufficient space needed for a large marine creature to roam undetected. However, the expansive Lake Winnebago might just be one exception to that rule. As Wisconsin's largest lake (whose boundaries are entirely in the state—

Lake Monsters of Wisconsin

sorry, Great Lakes), Winnebago enjoys over 85 miles of shoreline, and even though average water depth rarely exceeds 20 feet, the lake's 215 square miles of water affords plenty of spacious living quarters for nearly any animal.

Noted folklorists Robert Gard and L.G. Sorden included a wonderful origin story of the lake monster in their seminal book, *Wisconsin Lore*. The authors tell that the legend of the giant lake monster dates back to when the Winnebago Tribe (Ho-Chunk) had their villages perched along the shores of the lake. Legend tells of the lake monster's mammoth hunger for moose, elk, and deer, as it would often position itself in the river channel where it lay in wait for passing prey that often crossed over from stream to stream. As the unsuspecting animals made their way to the water, the beast would latch on and drag them under to their watery grave. By the time the monster had finished gorging on its capture, nothing of the animals remained. No hooves, no hair, and no horns. Unlike those predictable game animals, no Native would dare risk their life by crossing over at that deadly spot. After an untold number of years living off what it could kill, the monster's time came to an eventual end when several Natives discovered the carcass of the giant beast floating on the surface of the water. The beast was dead, and when examined, a huge sharp elk antler was discovered protruding from the beast's belly...deadly evidence that its greed had caused it downfall. Although the original behemoth is dead, Natives believe that descendants of this deadly creature continue to call Lake Winnebago home.

As nondescript tales of the large beast in Winnebago have swirled around for decades, few stories provided any actual specifics to accompany them. This lack of details works wonderfully for spinning a terrifying yarn around a blazing campfire, yet it does little to further the literature surrounding the mystery. One aspect of researching the paranormal that I truly love is the opportunity to really delve into the history of a certain location, and there is no greater mechanism for this than old local newspa-

The Lake Winnebago Water Beast

A close encounter with the beast

pers. These newspapers are time portals back to the early days of a community. There is no better feeling than spending the day scouring through the obituaries, town gossip, and local business adverts, in order to finally discover the rare headline that touts the town's folklore. For this case, that joy was provided to me by the April 14, 1887 edition of the *Oshkosh Daily Northwestern*, which proclaimed that the "First Sea Serpent" had been spotted. This almost fantastical tale tells of Mr. John McCabe, who, along with a Captain Lehman, reported seeing a gigantic animal swimming through the river in Winneconne (Winneconne waterway connects to Lake Winnebago). At first glance the story is seemingly farfetched—the witnesses estimated that the aquatic beast was about 30 feet high and "was something than 80 feet long" as it swam north. This article makes the sarcastic mention that the creature was in the area to check out George Peck's recently purchased summer resort.

After such a tantalizing account, the entire region must have been bursting with sea serpent fever, which would explain why it didn't take long for

Lake Monsters of Wisconsin

the mysterious creature to make another unsettling appearance. The April 28, 1887 edition of the *Oshkosh Daily Northwestern* proclaimed that "Another Sea Serpent" had been sighted in Lake Winnebago. The article recounts the story of Messrs. C.H. Forward and A.H. Gross who, while walking along the lake shore near Washington Street, "observed a curious looking animal in the water." About a mile from shore something unknown was splashing the water considerably as it moved in a northwesterly direction. Mesmerized by the beast's noisy onward course, the men felt certain that they had "never saw anything like it before." Of course, the level headed newspaper could not refrain from taking another jovial jab at the serpent sighting by adding "the serpent was evidently bound for Island Park where it will probably be the leading attraction this summer."

Sea serpent madness was now in a full frenzy. The very next day the *Oshkosh Daily Northwestern* covered yet another sighting of the now regular water visitor. This time the beast appeared to some boys who were

The mysterious Lake Winnebago

The Lake Winnebago Water Beast

down by the water spearing fish in the slough. The boys were "greatly alarmed" when an undulating monster broke the surface of the water exposing a "huge black body which resembled a large log." Even more amazingly, as the kids watched, a head soon followed the body out of the water, complete with a neck that was covered in a heavy mane which stretched "fully three feet in length" and resembled the weeds found near shore. It is not known whether the mane the kids saw was actually just tangled weeds strung around the beast's neck, or truly some sort of unique monster mane. The newspaper speculated that this creature was most likely the same one that had been spotted and reported in previous accounts.

Two years later the mystery of the wild serpent still continued to baffle residents. This time newspapers from around the country jumped in on the local legend. The July 22, 1889 edition of the *San Antonio Daily Light* claimed that finally, after several years of wild sightings in which witnesses described everything from a monster to a whale, the mystery could now be put to bed with the capture of a huge sea lion along the lakeshore. A much more detailed and interesting version of the terrific capture was printed in the July 22, 1889 edition of the *Milwaukee Weekly Wisconsin*. The story goes that back in 1885 (4 years prior), the famed Adam Forepaugh Circus had been in town showcasing it menagerie of exotic people, strange performers, and curious animals—several of which were giant caged sea lions. Before departing for the next town, the circus crew decided to give the sea lions a quick bath in Winnebago's "pure water" and transported the cage down to Menasha Driving Park. As the cage was being backed up into the water "one of the iron doors became disarranged and allowed the largest of the species to escape." Apparently the notion of a large sea lion escaping into a heavily used lake was quickly forgotten, because none of the previous sightings made any mention of a fugitive sea lion as the possible serpent solution. Fast forward four years to 1889. Two young boys spent the day spearing frogs near the frog farm when they spotted something so bizarre it forced them to dash into Menasha screaming wildly like banshees about seeing a whale in the lake. Like yelling fire in a crowded theater, the young men attracted quite a crowd with their unusual story, and soon a large posse of men armed to the teeth with "hooks, spears, and strong cords" ventured off to the location of the whale sighting. There, in the shallows of the water, was a huge sea lion desperately trying to free itself from the imprisonment of being grounded on the lake bottom. The men quickly wrapped the creature up in their cords and were able to safely wrangle it to shore. Once sprawled out on the banks of the lake, the true size of the beast could truly be appreciated. At over 11 feet in length and "fully eight feet in circumference" its entire skin was covered "with a short hair of a brownish color, but blackest on the tail and feet." At over 400 pounds, every movement the creature engaged in provided a new challenge for its captors. The hideous beast must have appeared like some freak of nature straight out of a bad science fiction book. A telegraph was swiftly sent off to Adam Forepaugh who instructed that the specimen be shipping back to him regardless of the expense. With the capture of the sea lion, the sea serpent nonsense could finally be put to rest. Well…not so quick.

Just like in every low-budget Hollywood horror movie scenario, where the slain monster always miraculously comes back from the dead, the mystery of the Winnebago serpent was only just beginning. The July 29, 1891 edition of the *Chicago Tribune* cast doubt on the idea that the sea lion was the only huge beast that called Lake Winnebago home. The newspaper covered the strange story of Mr. Herman Mass, a farmer from Chilton, Wisconsin who lived on the shores of the lake. One morning while out mowing the marsh, Mr. Mass came upon a giant female blacksnake lingering near the water. Fearing that he was witnessing some sort of supernatural mirage, Mass drew closer to the 11-foot-long beast. The paper doesn't include all the grisly details of the battle, but somehow the farmer was able to slay the mighty beast. The situation became more bizarre when Mass examined the snake's mouth and discovered "teeth an inch long." If the sight of the lengthy monster wasn't terrifying enough,

The Lake Winnebago Water Beast

Mass also claimed that "upwards of sixty of its young were taken from its body measuring from eight to twelve inches." Needless to say, the paper claimed that "no snake of its kind has ever been seen before hereabouts." Could this long snake be responsible for some of the serpent sightings? If it was indeed the culprit, it was by no means the only one.

If you happened to be wandering around Oshkosh in 1895, you could have stopped by Thomas Smith's butcher shop on Main Street to witness a truly giant monster that had been taken from Lake Winnebago. The November 7 edition of the *Oshkosh Daily Northwestern* provided all the details of this amazing catch, which was described as being the "largest, so far is known, that was ever caught in these waters." Of course, the creature on display was not a genuine sea serpent—at least not in the traditional sense—but it was, however, a monster in its own right. Hanging on the butcher's wall was a six-foot, 125-pound sturgeon that awed even the most seasoned fisherman of the area. In fact, many experienced anglers "who have seen big fish taken from these lakes have never seen any larger ones than the one now on exhibition." The addition of a giant sturgeon pulled from the lake only crowded the ever growing list of possible serpent explanations, a list that would soon expand even more.

Leave it to a deputy game warden to literally muddy the waters around the lake monster legend, because that is exactly what Capt. C.W. Johnston did with his discovery of a strange bone fossil dwelling on the lake bottom. The description given by the August 20, 1907 edition of the *Oshkosh Daily Northwestern* was "The thing at first glance looks like a long snout or nose." Being that the specimen had been found in a lake with a legend-filled past caused the immediate speculation that the discovery was a piece of fossilized bone remains from "a colossal sea serpent" that had been sighted so regularly in years past. Others in the community opined that the finding might be from "some huge creature that inhabited the North American continent during the stone age." Captain Johnston had been out on his boat patrolling for illegal gill nets when a strange piece of bone-like material lying in the shallow water along Long Point caught his eye. What ultimately became of this unique rare find remains unknown. The newspaper hinted that Captain Johnston might donate the bone structure to the library museum, yet through all my research I have not been able to track down the whereabouts of the mysterious fossil. Perhaps it is safely tucked away in someone's attic or basement, waiting to be rediscovered.

On May 12, 1911, the *Washington Post*, while reminiscing on the fading lore of sea serpents, inquired as to why the once often seen creatures seemed to all but disappear. The article mentions the case of the Lake Winnebago water monster. Casting doubt on the escaped circus animal theory, the paper wondered "just how they reconciled the particular sea lion with fresh water was not explained," nor did the sea lion explanation account for the beast surviving several harsh Wisconsin winters. Now a decade removed from the last reported sighting, the paper recounted several previously unknown stories that transpired during the height of the great Lake Winnebago scare, including that of resort employees who "were chased out of the water in the morning, and had to run for their lives" from the deadly serpent. If the paper's intention was to re-ignite the Lake Winnebago mystery, it did not succeed. For the past 20 years I have given numerous lectures in the towns and cities surrounding Lake Winnebago; without fail, each and every time I address the sea serpent legend of the lake, I am met with blank stares from the audience. Even many of the lifelong residents of the area are unfamiliar with the lake's dubious reputation. A couple years ago while investigating this legend I reached out to several historical societies in the region, inquiring about the legend of the lake in hopes that they may have some firsthand accounts tucked away in dusty journals or diaries. And while most of the historians expressed curiosity about the legend, none of them were able to provide any new insight. If some huge unknown beast is still roaming around in Lake Winnebago, it has done a magnificent job shielding itself from the prying eyes of the locals.

The Long Neck of Long Lake

Where To Encounter It

√ Long Lake is located along the cities of Dundee and Campbellsport. There are plenty of public places to encounter the beast, including the Long Lake Recreation Area. However, my favorite place to watch for the monster is Benson's Hide-A-Way in Campbellsport.

Creature Lore

Often while researching cases of the bizarre and unusual, we tend to believe that they are seemingly isolated events, but in actuality sometimes we discover that these events are tied to a whole slew of other strangeness. Such is the case of the monster in Long Lake, a location that for years has been infamous for its bizarre UFO sightings.

Sometime in 1989, two campers were out on the lake when a giant black and yellow, 25-foot creature with a head like a football emerged from the

Lake Monsters of Wisconsin

water—at least that is the story Bill Benson told to *Milwaukee Journal* reporter Betsy Thatcher. Benson is the long time proprietor of Benson's Hide-A-Way, a bar and grill that serves as a local meeting spot for UFO enthusiasts. Benson's is also the location for an annual UFO Daze festival, which draws out thousands of curious sky watchers looking to spot one of the frequently reported UFOs buzzing over Long Lake. When I spoke with Mr. Benson, he provided a few more details that the newspaper did not include. It was a nice summer day in 1989, when a young couple staying at Long Lake Recreation Area stopped into Din's Garage and Mini Mart with a terrifying story. The couple was out fishing, when suddenly they spotted a giant 25-foot eel-like monster swimming near the shore of the state park. The

Benson's UFO bar is home to many odd sightings

beast's skin was dark brown and covered with light brown spots, looking like nothing the couple had ever seen before. After a few fleeting moments, the creature dove back under the surface and disappeared from sight. The couple was so shaken by the experience that they vowed to never return to the lake.

Benson also told me about another odd phenomenon that happens quite frequently on the lake. On picturesque days when the lake is perfectly calm, and no boats can be found anywhere within sight, giant waves will suddenly appear in the middle of the lake as though created by some unseen source. These phantom waves are so powerful that they crash into

The Long Neck of Long Lake

the shore. Apparently, these mysterious waves have been spotted quite frequently, yet no visible cause for them has ever been determined.

In 1998, a local man wrote into the *Campbellsport News* about an odd sighting that occurred in Long Lake. The letter came from Bob Kuehn, a Campbellsport resident, who was affectionately known as "UFO Bob." According to Kuehn, a young woman was visiting the lake when she spotted a "huge dark object several hundred feet off shore." The creature moved through the water in an undulating motion, much like that of a snake. The motion caused waves so large that they made it to the shore of the lake, causing a loud crash. Most likely, Kuehn (now deceased) was recounting the story of Beth Quinn, who told of her strange encounter on Long Lake in an interview with the website *W-Files.com*. It was the summer of 1994 when Quinn saw a "big black swan type sea monster" moving out on the lake. She was close enough to the beast to see that it had a "dragon type face"—a face so odd that she was convinced that it could not be any known duck or swan, and that whatever she had witnessed was something she had never seen before in her entire life. As bad luck would have it, Quinn was alone during her incredible sighting. Looking for someone who could corroborate her story, she immediately ran to a nearby cabin to alert others of the mysterious beast. The excited group raced back to the shore, only to discover that whatever sort of creature she had seen, it was now nowhere to be found.

Bob also alluded to another sighting that involved a large salamander-like creature crossing Highway 67. When I inquired about this story, Bill Benson told me that the sighting occurred just south of Mr. Ed's Campground. The creature was described as a 3-foot-long beast that resembled a giant salamander. Many believed that it was somehow related to the creature(s) spotted in Long Lake, perhaps even a baby monster. Land sightings of odd creatures are fairly common in places that contain a lake monster legend. We tend to believe that these creatures are somehow completely confined to the water, yet many of them seem to be equally suited on land as well.

Lake Monsters of Wisconsin

On their own, the strange sea serpent sightings would be odd enough, but when you factor in all of the UFO sightings too, the area around Long Lake takes on a much more mysterious tone. For decades, reports of unidentified flying objects have been recorded around Long Lake. Over the years, hundreds of unusual lights, crafts, and other unknown objects have been seen flying and hovering over the area. All of these sightings have garnered the area the title of being the "UFO Capital of the World"—a title that it shares with two other Wisconsin cities (Belleville & Elmwood).

Even more weirdness from the area comes in the form of a crop circle found in the nearby Jersey Flats. In her book, *Monsters of Wisconsin*, intrepid researcher Linda Godfrey tells of a strange crop circle being discovered by some local farmers in the 1940s—long before most people had ever heard of crop circles.

Are all of these different phenomena at Long Lake somehow related? Or has Long Lake been a victim of its own publicity? The best way to answer these questions is to visit Long Lake and decide for yourself...the UFO Daze festival always runs during the third weekend of July.

The Monster in Devil's Lake

Where To Encounter It

Devil's Lake is really only accessible from Devil's Lake State Park.

Creature Lore

In the early days, Wisconsin was overflowing with state-wide reports of terrifying sea beasts. From the oral histories of the American Indians to the written reports of early settlers, people from all over Wisconsin were spotting these marine monsters in their lakes, rivers, and streams. Resort towns considered these sightings a boom for business, because vacationers flocked to the water for an opportunity to see these bizarre animals. These unusual sightings continued all the way through the 1920s and '30s, at which point they suddenly ceased. Whether people stopped seeing these

Lake Monsters of Wisconsin

beasts, or if the newspapers simply quit reporting on them, Wisconsin's sea serpents swiftly disappeared. Slowly, the deadly reputations of these creatures that had been building for decades began to fade into oblivion.

Since its discovery, Devil's Lake has been surrounded in mystery and legend. Even its name sparks intrigue among historians, who struggle to decipher its true meaning. The Winnebago named the lake *Ta-wa-cun-chuk-dah,* meaning "Sacred Lake." Other popular translations include: Holy Lake, Mystery Lake, Spirit Lake, Wild Beauty Lake, and Bad Spirit Lake. The name "Devil's Lake" seemed to be one of the more sensational translations accepted by the entrepreneurial business and tourism folks. The major obstacle in the translation lies with the lack of early records from the first settlers of the land. Studies of the area indicate that a band of Natives probably lived near the lake approximately 10,000 to 12,000 years ago. These early tribes were the ones responsible for the effigy mounds that are scattered throughout the park. Eventually the Winnebago Tribe settled in the region. According to the monograph *A Lake Where Spirits Live,* one of the earliest recorded sightings of the tribe came in 1846 when the pioneer physician, Dr. Charles Cowles, encountered a native fishing village along the lake.

The early natives told amazing tales of the lake's origin along with numerous other supernatural occurrences. Legend tells that the lake was formed when the giant thunderbirds (*Wakhakeera*) engaged in a heated battle with the water monsters (*Wakunja*) who lived in a den in the depths of the lake. The great birds flew high above the land and hurled their thunderbolts down into the waters; the water monster shot up giant rocks and waterspouts from the deeps of the lake. The fight raged on for days. The effects of the battle ravished the land, trees were blown down, rocks were split open, and the land was torn up. Finally, the thunderbirds prevailed and journeyed back to their nest in the north. It was said that no native dared approached the lake for quite some time. Although they lost the battle, not all of the water monsters were killed, and those survivors continue

The Monster in Devil's Lake

to live in Devil's Lake. A 1964 article in the *Capital Times* stated that for years "it was the custom of the early Indians to make tobacco offerings to the spirits of the lake."

Another legend of the lake tells of a green dragon that lived in the center of the lake. This all-powerful creature was equipped with seven heads and a body that no arrow could pierce. The natives believed that the dragon was the creator of the lake, and he demanded continual offerings which included an annual sacrifice of a fair maiden. The tribe became resentful of the creature's insatiable appetite for tributes and sought out a way to rid themselves of the greedy beast. The beast did have one weakness—his brain was located behind the left eye of his middle head, making it vulnerable to attack. A young brave named River-Child set off to challenge the beast. Along the way he encountered a group of natives who had also experienced the wrath of the dragon. They listened intently to his plan,

Fog settles in over Devil's Lake

and when he was done talking they reluctantly agreed to assist him. They waited until dusk, when the water began to swirl and the dragon began to surface. The braves all aimed their arrows at his eye. Sensing their ability to kill him, the dragon swam after River-Child, only to be captured in his net. After an exhausting battle, River-Child was finally able to best the beast with a swift swipe into the beast's eye. The beast may have been killed, but its spirit can be heard screaming for revenge at the onset of every storm.

With nearly 1.5 million annual visitors, Devil's Lake State Park enjoys the status of being Wisconsin most visited state park. Sadly, the majority of these visitors are unaware of the lake's mysterious past. During my research investigation at Devil's Lake, I was amazed by the beauty of the area. A heavy fog settled down over the lake as though it was trying to obscure its mysteries. The cold, fog, and feel of the place immediately transported me back to my research into a similar creature of Lough Ree, Ireland. But you don't have to travel over to the Emerald Isle to come face to face with a sea monster—you can just head out to Devil's Lake.

During my first expedition to Devil's Lake, I was hoping to find some strange serpent stories from some of the employees. In what has become an all too common situation while researching cases, I learned that no one from the nature center staff was aware of the lake's supernatural reputation. Luckily, with some persistence, I finally was passed along to the Seasonal Naturalist, Diane Pillsbury, who provided me with a wealth of folklore on the lake.

Devil's Lake stands out from most other serpent hotspots because of the sheer number of different beasts thought to dwell in the waters. Unlike most places that claim to have one type of water beastie, if you believe the reports, Devil's Lake is home to a couple of entirely different monsters.

The Monster in Devil's Lake

One octopus-type creature sighting is documented in Scott Francis' book, *Monster Spotters*, where Francis tells of an old Sioux legend. One day a group of eager young braves gathered to depart on a hunting expedition. Just as the canoes were launched, the water around them began to swirl, and in an instant the bubbles exploded into a thrashing of tentacles that quickly arose from the chaos. Before the men could even react, several braves found themselves helplessly tangled in the beast's deadly tentacles. As the monster finally submerged, it took the screaming braves with it. All of the commotion had attracted the attention of the rest of the tribe, which quickly rushed down to the shore, only to witness the watery graves that awaited the sinking tribesmen. These deaths led the tribesmen to use extreme caution when approaching the lake, afraid that the beast would wreak havoc on them, too.

In his book, *Monster Hunt*, Rory Storm writes about a legend in which the Nakota Tribe encountered a plesiosaur-type monster. The lake was reeling from a long drought that had dried up major portions of the water.

Many Natives were said to have lost their lives in the lake

Lake Monsters of Wisconsin

While out on a morning trek, several tribesmen spotted a huge fish-like creature called a *Hokuwa* that had become trapped on the semi-muddy bottom of the drying lake bed. The hideous looking creature was described as having a very large body with an elongated neck that stretched out to its small head. Even the bravest among the tribe would not get within striking distance of the monster. After a bit, the beast was able to flap its body free and descended back into the depths of the lake. This report would seem to indicate that the creature encountered resembled the common sightings of a plesiosaur-type beast that are frequent at Loch Ness or Lake Champlain.

A few years later on July 11, 1892, the *Chicago Tribune* again reported another plesiosaur-type serpent sighting. The article tells that on July 10th, at around 8pm Col. B.C. Deane "a man of unquestionable veracity," L.E. Hoyt, J.B. Cundah, and F.E. Shults, were out fishing:

The party was fishing at the southwest part of the lake, near the marsh, and having good luck at that spot concluded to anchor their boats and set their lines. They had done this, and were about to partake of refreshments when a peculiar rippling of the water was noticed about 100 feet distant. Up to this time the water had remained perfectly placid, and this strange disturbance attracted their attention. Gazing in that direction they soon saw the head of an immense reptile as it appeared above the water where the disturbance was first noticed. At first the head was barely visible above the water, but gradually it rose until it stood fully six feet out of the water, and to the part of the body that was at the surface of the water two large fin-like paddles were attached. The reptile did not seem to take the least notice of the fishermen, but its large head swayed from side to side, looking in an opposite direction as if in search of something. It was not long before the object of its search appeared. It was nothing less than a second sea serpent of exactly the same description. The second one made its appearance in the same manner as the first. She stood motionless for a few seconds and then the first one made a terrific plunge toward the other and

The Monster in Devil's Lake

the two serpents were in mortal combat. They lashed the water to such an extent that the waves came near swamping the boats and the party, pale as death, cut them loose and rowed ashore. Today a party of hunters was organized and started in search of the monsters.

The 1892 sighting was covered in many newspapers around the country. The *Xenia Daily Gazette* of Ohio wrote that "two indescribable monsters appeared in Devil's Lake." The reputation of the lake being a place of unnatural events started to spread. One of the first unofficial sea serpent researchers of Devil's Lake was a Chicago man, W.S. Grubb. On July 11, 1897, the *Chicago Tribune* reported that Grubb "spent many of summer here, is daily on the lookout for a large sea serpent which usually makes its appearance the first week of July, but has failed to show up for the season."

Devil's Lake seems to have been affected by the same slowing of sea serpent reports that the rest of the state has experienced over the decades. One would think that with well over 1 million annual visitors, someone would encounter the beast of the lake. However, it should be mentioned that many people who encounter something paranormal tend to keep that information to themselves, in fear that no one will believe them. I have also had people share their stories with me that they have kept secret for 10, 20 or 30 years, because they just didn't know who to tell. My own expeditions to Devil's Lake came up empty-handed, but I can only hope that, if the beasts still do dwell in the lake, someone will eventually encounter them.

A Mystery in Lake Superior

Where To Encounter It

The best opportunity to visit Lake Superior is along the northern part of Wisconsin from Superior to Ashland and east along Highway 2.

Creature Lore

The height of sea serpent reports came in the 1800s and early 1900s. During this period our lakes and oceans remained mostly unexplored, and the bodies of water possessed unlimited amounts of danger, romance, and deadly creatures that dwarfed anything ever seen before. The sheer uniqueness of these creatures was limitless with tourists, fisherman, boat captains, and nearly everyone else who was in a frenzy over what lurked beneath the waters. Somewhere around the 1930s, reports of sea serpents started to dwindle. Whether people stopped seeing them or the media

A Mystery in Lake Superior

stopped reporting them, serpent sightings all but vanished from the public's awareness, leaving a giant mystery in their place. Where did all of these creatures go? Did they move deeper to avoid the approach of man, or had they simply become extinct? For decades, reports of serpents remained a rare phenomenon. Yet recently, for some inexplicable reason, sea serpents sightings are again on the rise, leading many legend trippers to grab their cameras and head off to Lake Superior in search of the next great serpent sighting.

The history of majestic Lake Superior is full of tales of something large and deadly inhabiting the seemingly unending body of water. Long before white pioneers settled the area, American Indians had already developed a healthy respect for the vicious creatures that dwelled in the lake. Oral tales from the Natives told of unimaginably huge beasts that could swallow a man, or ship, with ease. If, for any reason, members of a tribe turned up missing, the disappearance was blamed on the serpents of the water. When white pioneers finally moved into the area, the once exclusively oral tales shifted to the widely circulated newspaper, which in turn spread the tales of the serpents much further than ever before.

On August 3, 1895, the *Ironwood News Record* wrote of the sensational sighting of the S.S. Curry during its trip down from Ashland, Wisconsin. The ship, under the direction of the "veracious" Captain George Robarge, was passing by White Fish Point at sunset when Robarge eyed a huge reptile that "thrust his long neck about the water's surface" a mere 400 yards from the ship. For a full five minutes the beast kept pace with the boat, allotting the ship's crew enough time to grab their "glasses" and obtain a better look. With binoculars in hand, the crew could make out an extraordinarily large creature whose neck "was some 15 feet in length" with jaws that parted a good foot or more. The article stated that the men watched with trepidation as "every now and then its body partially rose above the waves and revealed a strange undulating motion" before disappearing into the dark of the water.

Lake Monsters of Wisconsin

In 1897, the *Detroit News-Tribune* reported on a terrifying attack from a creature believed to be a giant squid. It happened as a ship was nearing the shallow waters around Duluth and struck what was thought to be a rock. One of the crewmen went to assess the damage of the collision when he tripped over a rope and landed in 10 feet of water. Immediately he was seized by the tentacles of a 70-foot green beast with "great scales and a forked tail." As his boat was being pushed out to sea the man appeared doomed to meet his fate as the creature's powerful grip tightened around his waist, sucking away his remaining air. As the man thrashed about, fighting to gain footing on the lake bottom, he could make out the beast's two giant eyes. After a mighty struggle, the brave sailor somehow broke free and made his way to shore, happy to have survived his encounter with the unknown beast.

The lake is home to reports of phantom ships, UFOs, and sea monsters

A Mystery in Lake Superior

The Lake Superior region of Wisconsin is an extremely popular destination for tourists looking to relax near the Great Lakes. As one of the state's most visited areas, a lot of eyes are cast onto the lake. It may come as no surprise that with so many people admiring the beauty of the water, sightings of the unexplained are bound to pop up.

Regardless of their belief in the paranormal, the majority of people who visit Lake Superior leave the area with the belief that it is a magical and mystical place. Some believe this is caused by the calm and soothing sounds of the waves crashing against the shore, while others experience a deeper, more spiritual, connection to the lake. As the largest of the Great Lakes, Superior offers plenty of space for weirdness to happen, and the overwhelming majority of cases aren't of sea serpents, but of phantom ships. It only seems logical when you consider that thousands of ships and crewmembers have met their end at the hands of the treacherous lake. Tales of tragic mishaps and disappearances are all too numerous on the unforgiving lake that has sent many sailors to their watery graves where they are doomed to spend eternity. The problem lies in the fact that these victims, along with their ships, are not resting peacefully. In fact, each year dozens of unsuspecting vacationers report seeing the ghostly images of old 1800s looking ships sailing across the lake. And even though nothing beats the picture of these ghostly vessels moving silently through a fog-filled moonlit night, sightings of these phantom ships have been reported in both day and night, with or without fog.

Outside of all the phantom ship sightings, sea serpents regularly get spotted as well. In their book, *The Mysterious North Shore*, authors William Mayo and Kate Barthel tell of a man who was visiting the area when he saw something he just couldn't explain. The man was checking out a spot near Stuart River, where he had discovered a good view overlooking the river and lake. Standing on a small cliff, the man noticed something in the lake that did not quite fit, explaining that he had seen something akin to a "really big fish or something" in the lake. Pressed for details, the man reported that it "looked like a rock at first—or a turtle's back." A bit confused by what he had experienced, the man continued with his story, claiming that the creature "would submerge, and you could just make it out under the surface, then it would move around and come back up." Trying to estimate the size of the mysterious creature, the man spread out his arms as wide as they would go, indicating that whatever it was that he saw, it was pretty big. Sticking with the common response of a typical witness, the man quickly tried to explain away his sighting as nothing more than a misidentification by telling himself it had to simply be a big fish or turtle—because what else could it be?

In 2013, after finishing a lecture in Minnesota, I was approached by a gentleman who wanted to share something odd that happened to him while at the dentist. The dental clinic that this man visited was located near Two Harbors, Minnesota, along Highway 61, which provides a wonderful view of the lake. The clinic had wisely positioned many of the chairs so that they would provide the patient with a relaxing view of Lake Superior. As

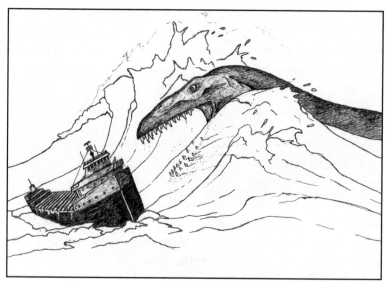

The monster of the lake was deemed a deadly killer

A Mystery in Lake Superior

the man sat and waited for the dentist to come in, he noticed what appeared to be a dolphin-like creature bobbing around in the water. Taking a closer look, the patient quickly realized that the beast was far too large to be a dolphin. The creature actually looked like a giant humped sea serpent. The man quickly leapt from his seat and rushed closer to the window—just in time to watch as the large mysterious creature dove under the surface and did not reappear. Of course, the patient kept his sighting to himself, thinking that the staff would believe he was crazy.

Each year I continue to receive a handful of reports from Lake Superior. Usually these reports originate from someone who was only able to catch a fleeting glimpse of something that seemed out of place in the lake. Mostly, these sightings lack any real details due to their short exposure. They end up in my unexplained pile—due to the insufficient details, it is difficult to place them in a category. It is not the fault of the eyewitnesses; it is just that these exposures happen so quickly that a perfect picture cannot be etched into our memory. I myself have spent a lot of time out on Lake Superior in search of sea serpents, and many things have caught my eye as I've scanned the water…unfortunately none of them turned out to be a sea serpent.

✓On your next trip to Lake Superior, you may want to avert your eyes from the water and focus on the sky, because a lot of UFOs have also been seen flying over the lake. Tales of mysterious buzzing lights, hovering objects, and unknown aircraft are plentiful along the lake. With reports of phantom boats, giant monsters lurking in the water, and UFOs flying overhead, you may just find yourself joining the long list of those who believe there is something truly magical about Lake Superior.

Pepie: The $50,000 Lake Monster

Where To Encounter It

Lake Pepin runs for 23 miles along the Mississippi River on Wisconsin's western border with Minnesota There are a plethora of locations for you to launch your boat, swim, or just watch beautiful Lake Pepin.

Creature Lore

Something unknown is lurking in Lake Pepin, and for over 140 years this mysterious creature has inhabited the largest lake on the Mississippi River. Just what this bizarre monster is remains unknown, as accounts seem to vary from witness to witness. The American Indians believed that it was a dangerous killer, the old pioneers believed it was an undiscovered species, and modern vacationers see it as a tourist draw. Each year the long list of eyewitnesses continues to grow, while the answer to what this puzzling creature really is remains as far away as it ever has.

Tales of the expansive lake hosting some unknown water beastie date back to the American Indians who first settled near the area. Legend tells of the Natives holding a healthy respect for the many mysteries of the lake. Their respect eventually turned to avoidance after numerous canoes were attacked and punctured by some large water beast. The beautiful waters of Lake Pepin quickly gained the reputation of a place that housed something dark and deadly.

Although oral tales of the creatures date back much further, the first recorded sighting of the creature took place on April 24, 1871. According to the April 26 edition of the *Wabasha County Sentinel*, local residents Giles Hyde and C. Page Bonney reported seeing a large unidentified marine monster in the lake. The sensational sighting reported that the creature was between the size of an elephant and a rhinoceros, and it moved with great rapidity. The newspaper also stated that on several prior occasions the creature had also been spotted, but no further details were given. The possibilities of the true origin of the creature were endless; the paper even speculated that "the water in the lake is known to be very deep, whales might live in—but this is not likely to be a whale." Other newspapers picked up and expanded on the case, as the *Titusville Herald* out of Pennsylvania stated that Lake Pepin was "infested with a marine monster." While no definitive explanation of the creature was purposed, two aspects of the monster were widely agreed upon—it was big, and it was fast.

In 1875, the creature made several other spectacular appearances. The *Pierce County Herald* told of a couple of strange sightings that took place in July. The details of the first sighting are lacking, as unfortunately the paper only states that a monster of some kind was spotted opposite Lake City, Minnesota. The second account is a bit more detailed and tells of Mr. Hewitt and two boys who were out sailing from Lake City to Wacouta in a skiff, when about halfway to their destination, a "dark, strange-looking

Lake Monsters of Wisconsin

object rose out of the lake about six feet high at the stern of the boat." The beast remained out of the water long enough for the trio to get a detailed look at it before it disappeared into the depths of the lake. Again, the paper failed to list specific details such as its color, type of body, or other identifying marks. And while most of the town was buzzing with the monster news, not all were believers in Pepie. Several skeptical residents believed that the mysterious sighting was nothing more than a regular lake occupant of natural origin, similar to the four-foot-long, five-and-a-half-pound eel that had been captured in the lake just prior to the sighting.

Throughout the early 1900s, the sea serpent legend calmed down a bit and, like most legends, it was nearly forgotten. It wasn't until more recent sightings started occurring that the rich history of the lake brought the creature back into the limelight.

Having been on several expeditions in search of the Loch Ness Monster, I was immediately struck by the uncanny similarities that Lake Pepin shares with the infamous Scotland Loch. Both bodies of water are approximately 23 miles long, both are over a mile wide, and both are surrounded by beautiful bluffs. Although Lake Pepin is not quite as deep as Loch Ness, there is still plenty of room for aquatic mysteries to live. And while many experts believe that Loch Ness does not have a sufficient food source to sustain a population of large sea serpents, Lake Pepin is widely recognized for its plentiful fishing and would have no problem providing for a family of creatures.

Adding even more credibility to the sea serpent legend is the fact that throughout history Lake Pepin's large body of water has been filled with

> Lake Pepin, Minn., is infested with a marine monster, between the size of an elephant and a rhinoceros, which moves through the water with great rapidity.

Newspaper accounts date back to the 1860s

Pepie: The $50,000 Lake Monster

Photo of "Pepie" taken by local fisherman Steve Raymond

many other large aquatic animals. On August 10, 1891, the *Eau Claire Weekly Leader* ran the headline, "A Big Fish." The story told of a shovel-nosed sturgeon that had been caught in Lake Pepin. The sturgeon's 16 pound head was described as the largest head ever seen in the area. The fish itself weighed well over 85 pounds. Certainly a fish of this size could have caused quite a disturbance on the lake, leading many to believe that the sturgeon was solely responsible for many of the sea serpent sightings.

The February 2, 1918 edition of the *La Crosse Tribune and Leader Press* featured a story of a mammoth sheephead fish being netted out of Lake Pepin. While a normal sized sheephead in the lake averaged one and a quarter pounds, this whopper weighed over 24 pounds. Even more remarkable than the weight was the sheer size of the fish, which measured over three feet long and had a girth of over one foot. If seen at the right distance, this giant sheephead certainly could have seemed like a large serpent.

Lake Monsters of Wisconsin

In 2011, a gentleman contacted me looking to report a strange sighting that he had at Lake Pepin back in the 1970s while fishing with his two young children. Without a boat, the trio was forced to fish off of a rock jetty along the Wisconsin side of the lake. They were about half-way out on the jetty when "something lunged up breaking the surface of the water." Gray in color, the fisherman estimated it to be one foot in diameter while about three feet of its body showed above the water. At first the man believed it was a Muskie, however its mouth was "open in such a way as to resemble an open pipe." The reason for its surfacing became clear as a bird flying three feet over the water was snatched out of mid-air by the mysterious creature.

Is this the monster of Lake Pepin?

Pepie: The $50,000 Lake Monster

The official Pepie website showcases several of the more interesting sightings that have been complied over the years. One such sighting took place on July 9, 2008. At approximately 10am, a motorist was traveling along on Highway 61 and noticed a very large creature moving parallel to the Lake City Beach. The witness pulled over to snap a photo of the creature, which was estimated to be somewhere between 30 and 40 feet long. After snapping the photo, the witness watched the creature slowly disappear back into the water.

On one of my expeditions to Lake Pepin, I spoke with a woman who vividly remembered her bizarre sighting of Pepie. On August 21, 2010, the woman and her husband were traveling along Highway 61 when something odd caught her attention. From the passenger window, she gazed out at Lake Pepin and noticed something moving in the water that resembled the long neck and head of a serpent. Not quite believing what she was seeing, the woman jokingly told her husband that she had just seen something that looked like Pepie. Her husband briefly turned his attention from the road to the lake and spotted the same creature. The couple estimated that—whatever the creature was—it had a neck and head that was sticking a good two feet out of the water. It also appeared that the head was attached to a larger body that was mostly submerged under the water. The sighting only lasted a few seconds, and the heavy traffic on the highway forced the couple to keep moving. It all happened so fast that they were not truly sure if they could believe their own eyes. The couple discussed the possibility that what they had seen was a dead log or other floating debris, and like so many others who have witnessed something strange in Lake Pepin, the couple chalked their sighting up as an unsolved mystery.

It is safe to say that the various fish listed above undoubtedly accounted for some of the sightings throughout the years. Yet, it is equally safe to say to state that based on the sheer size and scope of the beast reported by eyewitnesses that something other than a few large fish has been living in the depths of Lake Pepin. Much to their credit, the town of Lake City has

Lake Monsters of Wisconsin

embraced the legend of Pepie. In fact, the downtown store of Treats & Treasures is an Official Pepie Watch Station and contains a lot of Pepie merchandise. I spoke with the shop's owner, who informed me that over the years many people have ventured into her store with their personal Pepie sightings. Local business owner Larry Nielson runs the Pepie website and is a wealth of knowledge on the history and sighting of the creature. Nielson and the town are so convinced that Pepie is real that they are offering a $50,000 reward to anyone who can capture proof of its existence.

The Pewaukee Lake Intruder

Where To Encounter It

Pewaukee Lake is located in Pewaukee. The downtown has a wonderful public beach and viewing area that make for a perfect monster hunting base camp.

Creature Lore

In the late 1800s, the resorts around Pewaukee Lake were bustling with a diverse array of visitors. Wealthy Chicagoans, vacationing families, avid fisherman, and locals looking to escape the heat, all took refuge at the beautiful lake. As the years went by, stories of the lake being inhabited by some sort of sea serpent were passed down from generation to generation like a precious family heirloom.

Lake Monsters of Wisconsin

The legend of the monster began slowly. Each summer, witnesses would recount their sightings over the crackling of a campfires. While most who listened deemed these tales as nothing more than exaggerated yarns meant to scare the children and terrify the faint of heart, year after year, the culmination of these summer tales began to take root. Suddenly, stories that were once considered fanciful tall tales were now seen as cautionary tales meant to protect unaware boaters and swimmers. Charles Brown claimed that witnesses often saw a huge "green thing" moving across the water with great rapidity. Others told Brown that the beast moved like "a gray streak" as it swam up and down the lake. On several occasions, the beast's head could be seen bobbing above the surface while "spouting a stream of water."

Apparently, the beast also had a strong penchant for the "well-patronized" resorts, as these were the areas that produced the most sightings. Skeptics claimed that the lake creature was devised by the resorts' dubious mar-

Waters where the legend was born

The Pewaukee Lake Intruder

Strange Catch—This 'Fish' Has Feet!

A 1971 newspaper article sparked more mystery

keting agents in an obvious attempt to fill more rooms. Conversely though, it seems pretty logical that most of the sightings would take place near the places that had the most people.

As the legend gained traction, a reward was offered to anyone who could capture the water beast. Neither the dollar amount, nor the specific details of the reward are known, but no one seemed willing to face the monster in order to cash in on the reward. One brave soul who found himself face to face with the monster hurled a spear at it, only to have it bounce off as though it struck a large rock or iron plate.

Nearly everything that is known about the Pewaukee Lake Intruder is attributable to Charles Brown. Granted, you would never know this by reading the many newspaper articles, books, and websites that frequently "borrow" his work without any sort of credit given. Perhaps borrowing from Brown is so prevalent because little other documentation about the monster has been discovered.

Usually a local historic society is a treasure trove of information for those seeking answers. Not only does it function as a warehouse of local history, containing newspaper files, artifacts, and plenty of local books, but I have found that a lot of members have lived in the community for most of their lives and possess a thorough knowledge of local history. Sadly, each historian I spoke with had never heard so much as a whisper about a sea monster in the lake. Word of my sea serpent interest quickly spread through the historical society members, prompting one member to contact me. This member had spent years searching the old newspaper archives while working on various projects, yet she had never stumbled across any mention of a sea monster in Pewaukee Lake. I, too, failed to find as much as

Lake Monsters of Wisconsin

a mere mention of some uninvited sea creature lurking in the lake. The only remotely close thing I found came from a 1971 article in the *Racine Journal Times Sunday Bulletin* which told of a two-and-a-half-foot long alligator being caught in the lake.

Over the years, I have given several lectures in the Pewaukee area, and I always used them as an opportunity to pan for lake monster information—unfortunately most of time I received a room full of blank stares. This case is filled with unanswered questions…mainly, is the reward still active, what happened to that spear, where did the monster go, and why did nearly all traces of its existence disappear?

Red Cedar Lake Monster

Where To Encounter It

There are two Red Cedar Lakes in Wisconsin. This one is located in with southern part of the state, between the cities of Oakland and Rockdale. It is part of the Red Cedar Lake State Natural Area and just south of Lake Ripley.

The lake is hard to access by car. From Cambridge, take Highway 12 to the east for twelve miles and then turn right on Brosig Lane (a small access road). The lake is best accessed by a canoe or kayak, or for the very brave, swimming.

Lake Monsters of Wisconsin

Creature Lore

In my nearly 20 years of researching the paranormal, I have heard a lot of sea serpents stories. I have dug up hundreds of newspaper reports from all over the world, and after a while a lot of these stories start to blend together in their similarities. What I love about the Red Cedar Lake stories is that the creature is not so much a sea serpent as it is a killing machine that devours unwary prey.

Looking at Red Cedar Lake today, it is hard to imagine that it was once home to some of the most exciting sea serpent encounters in Wisconsin. The main problem with the idea is the shallowness of the lake. According to the Wisconsin DNR, the lake's maximum depth is around 6 feet, while over ninety percent of the lake is less than 3 feet deep. This doesn't leave a lot of room for an eighty- foot monster to maneuver. Yet, back in the

A perfect setting for a monster?

Red Cedar Lake Monster

1800s the lake was described as a much deeper body of water, which years of low rainfall and runoff all but drained. Little of the land surrounding the lake has changed, as it is still mostly comprised of farmland, making the lake hard to reach by car. In 1984, the lake was designated a State Natural Area and is currently owned by the Wisconsin DNR.

Out of all the serpent stories featured in this book, the Red Cedar Lake encounters rank as some of my favorites. Throughout the book, you will read a lot of stories of witnesses who engaged in bloody battles with lake monsters—everything from a man smashing a serpent with his oar, a fisherman stabbing a serpent, and even a witness firing his gun at a serpent. This case, however, is the only one where the serpent takes revenge on anything and everything that it can.

On August 15, 1890, the *Oshkosh Daily Northwestern* described a deadly encounter with the beast. A Red Cedar Lake farmer was horrified as he watched a "reptile forty feet long carry off one of his hogs." The paper speculated that the deadly lake monster was the same creature that had been spotted in 1880, when it was only ten feet in length.

It didn't take long for the creature to receive a deadly reputation as a ferocious killer. This well-earned reputation was only enhanced by the media reports of the day. One of my favorite articles came on September 5, 1891, when the *Janesville Gazette* ran this entertaining piece:

> The cedar lake sea serpent is again making trouble. When first seen, about ten years ago, the serpent was variously estimated at from thirty to forty feet in length, but now it cannot be less than eighty feet long. This year it has been particularly destructive of young pigs and lambs which might be feeding near the banks of the lake, sometimes running nearly half the length of its body on the land to seize its prey. It has never been seen

but once with its body entirely upon land, and some doubts are expressed as to the truthfulness of this report, as the man who claims to have been an eyewitness of this occurrence is not noted for his truth and voracity. It is generally seen just at the close of the day or very early in the morning; and when seen with head raised ten feet from the surface of the water, its mouth wide open, and rushing towards the shore, its appearance is apt to carry consternation to the stoutest nerves. When it comes to curiosities, this section of Wisconsin is bound not to be undone by any other part of the state.

In his monograph, *Sea Serpents*, Folklorist Charles E. Brown wrote of an interesting 1891 encounter. He tells of a fisherman who had just returned home and was tying up his boat. He looked out into the lake and saw a large form undulating through the water. It appeared to be a large snake or fish with its head submerged under the water. The astonished man watched as the creature swam out of sight. Excited, the fisherman told several of his friends and neighbors, only to discover that others had seen the bizarre marine monster as well. One neighbor described the beast as having a large head with several saw tooth-looking protuberances running down the spine of its back.

The story of the Red Cedar Monster changed in 1891, when locals believed that there existed an underground water passage linking Red Cedar Lake with Lake Ripley to the north. Low rainfall had made Red Cedar Lake extremely shallow. When sightings began to increase in the deeper Lake Ripley, several newspapers picked up on the rumor that the creature had run out of prey at Red Cedar Lake and traveled up to Lake Ripley. The *Janesville Gazette* wrote, "Residents of the banks of the latter lake are positive that they have caught glimpse of his snakeship."

Red Cedar Lake Monster

✓ *The lake monster was blamed for numerous cattle deaths*

If the monster did travel to Lake Ripley, it wasn't gone long, because on June 16, 1892 the *Pocahontas County Sun* ran the article "A Serpentine Monster," telling of several Germans who were out boating on Red Cedar when they spotted a floating log sticking several feet out of the water. The group watched as a large mud turtle climbed upon the log to sun itself, and it turned out that the perceived log was actually a large lake monster. Instead of enjoying some rays, the turtle disappeared into the creature's "capacious mouth." The lake monster must have had a ravenous appetite that wasn't limited to turtles. At the same time the Germans spotted the creature, *Waterloo Daily Courier* claimed that local farmer, Will Ward, had several of his valuable sheep fall victim to the monster, writing, "Their mangled forms were found in the mud, partly devoured."

However, it should be noted that not everybody was a true believer in the serpent. On August 24, 1894, the *Marshfield Times* poked a bit of fun at the serpent. The area was in the midst of a heat wave that had turned the water of the lake into a "mass of jelly." The paper joked that the jelly must have been caused by the melting of the lake's sea serpent from the extreme heat.

Lake Monsters of Wisconsin

As previously mentioned, the lake is very hard to access without a boat of some kind. As I circled the lake in my car, I did find several high spots on the road that made for a good serpent watching post, but to really see the lake you need to use an access road and get in closer. The lake itself is a pretty good size (370 acres) and is surrounded by wetlands and marshy water that also inhibits easy access. The access road (Brosig Lane) does a good job at getting you to the lake. As I was exploring the lake by myself, my mind started to explore the idea that because the lake was so shallow, a person could almost walk right across the entire thing without having to swim at all. I scoured the area in search of the deadly monster, but once again I came up empty-handed. Regretfully, I did not end up walking across the lake…which is probably why I am still alive today.

The Rock River Visitor

Where To Encounter It

The Rock River begins in Brandon, Wisconsin and winds its way 300 miles south through Illinois and Iowa. There are numerous towns in Wisconsin along the Rock River for you to discover your own monster sighting.

Creature Lore

Most legends do not magically spring up overnight. Instead they often slowly build, progress, and morph over the span of decades as each new telling propels them further into the public psyche. The origin of the Rock River monster started with the Winnebago Tribe which often camped along the banks of the river. Their oral tales told of a humungous and terrible water monster inhabiting the waterway. Around fires, tribesman would colorfully describe the demon as being a huge snake-like serpent, complete with great deadly jaws and razor sharp claws. Large horns protected its head, and its long thin body and tail could stretch out over the entirety of the river. Although actual Native sightings of the beast were pretty rare, evidence of its existence was often seen in the great churning and boiling commotion stirred up in the waters. Believing that three different serpents all called the river home, tribes approached the water with great caution. They believed the demon was not only responsible for the frequent capsizing of canoes, but that it was the sole reason why so many people never returned from their visit to the water. Every year, in the warming spring weather, the sounds of the monster breaking up the final remnants of winter's ice could be heard far and wide. In 1950, the *Wisconsin State Journal* expounded on the Native legends, telling of the common belief that the monster had numerous dens carved in the deepest part of the river, where "it slept and to which it took its victims for devouring." If river use was deemed absolutely necessary, tobacco and other offerings were placed in the water with the hope that they would allow the tribes to return to the shore in one piece.

To explain away lake monsters, skeptics often turn to alligators as being the cause and culprit of many sightings. While this limited theory can by no means solve every monster sighting, for the case of Rock River, they may actually be on to something—I have dug up enough alligator stories to convince me that there must have been an alligator breeding farm somewhere along the river. In February of 1892, a five-and-a-half-foot alligator was found dead a mere 20 feet from the Rock River. The *Janesville Gazette* surmised that the huge saurian was a circus escapee that found its way into the river, and upon finding that the snow filled February waters were not to its liking, it slithered out in hopes of sunning itself on the riverbank. Unfortunately, the freezing winter winds provided little warmth, and the beast quickly perished. Soon after it died, the gator was discovered by L. Hart, a local farmer, who speedily brought the beast into Milton, where plans to stuff it began. Later, in July of 1892, another alligator made an appearance in Rock River. The *Janesville Gazette* claimed that a scaly alligator was making its home under the Jeffris building. For several nights in a row, witnesses spotted the alligator thrashing its tail about the water. Just where the scaly creature came from, the paper did not say.

The Rock River Visitor

The long river would provide plenty of hiding spaces for something large

In September of 1903, two brothers, Will and George Berger, were playing alongside the river at Spring Brook when they noticed a strange looking lizard crawl of the water and slither onto a log. Terrified, the boys ran home and enlisted the aid of their older brother, Otto Berger, who grabbed his rifle, darted back to the river, and found the creepy creature still sunning itself on the log. Otto told the *Janesville Daily Gazette* that he took deliberate aim and shot the beast right behind the ear. When the carcass was retrieved the brothers were in possession of a three-foot long alligator, which they promptly—and proudly—put on display at their home. In June of 1918, John A. Hazelwood lost one of his prized pets, which just happened to be an alligator. The creature was placed in its sleeping box for the night, and when dawn approached, the beast was nowhere to be found. Tracks that the alligator left behind in the dirt were eventually followed down to the Rock River, where the beast seemed to have found its freedom.

Sightings of alligators in Rock River continued to modern times, too. In 2005, a 2-foot alligator was sunning itself near Theresa, Wisconsin, when it was shot and killed by Police Chief Michael Simmons, who responded to a call from a concerned citizen. Wisconsin Department of Natural Resources employee Christian Simmons told the *Beaver Dam Daily Citizen* that this was most likely a case of "an irresponsible pet owner letting this thing go in the river."

Through the years, stories of the river monster seemed to ebb and flow right along with the river's current, but the core stories were never entirely forgotten. In 1940, memories of the legend came flooding back when a deadly beast was once again spotted along the shoreline of the Rock River. We often think of trained observers as being the most reliable eye witnesses. Whether they are police officers, pilots, or firefighters, those in respected positions—where being alert and attentive to details can literally be a life or death matter—tend to enjoy higher presumed credibility. This type of thinking is what makes the 1940 sightings by three police officers considerably more interesting. Fortunately, the September 7 edition of the *Madison Capital Times* documented the entire event. It was a normal September day as Motorcycle Officer Ray Brier stopped along a Watertown bridge overlooking the river and noticed something large sunning itself down on the riverbank. When he returned to the police station, Brier was reluctant to tell of his odd sighting, fearing that his fellow officers would think he was nuts. Noticing Brier's sincerity, officers E.C. Knight and Herbert Schwantes were persuaded to go to the river to see the monster for themselves. Together, all three officers made their way to the river and soon discovered that there was indeed a beast on the loose. Officer Knight was able to get a clear look at the beast through his field glasses, telling the newspaper that the creature was "about six feet long, with a large head from which protruded two knoblike eyes." The body "was snakelike and it had two humps that coiled above the water." Intrigued by the officers' report, townsfolk quickly began flocking to the river in search of the new arrival. Not to be disappointed, many sight seekers returned with their own sighting of the mysterious visitor.

The Rock River Visitor

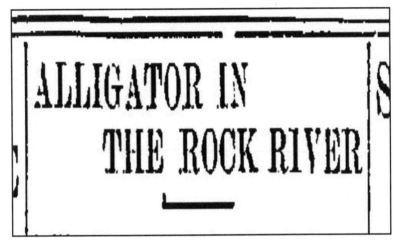

Many alligators have found their way into the river

Like so many other tales of contemporary lake monsters, the mysterious case of the Rock River visitor was never officially solved. Some will believe that gators are solely to blame, others will cling to stories of extremely large carp or sturgeon, while still others will place all of the blame firmly on witness misidentification. Yet regardless of all the competing theories, and with the stark realization that the true identity of the beast may never be discovered, one can take comfort and solace in knowing the legend will continue to blossom and grow for many generations to come.

Rocky:
The Rock Lake Terror

Where To Encounter It

Rock Lake is just outside of Lake Mills. The lake has ample viewing areas including Sandy Beach and Tyranena Park.

Creature Lore

Rock Lake is one of those unique places where several different legends combine to create a supernatural mystique that completely envelops the entire area. The origin of the lake monster (often referred to as Rocky) dates back to the first Native people that made their home along the water, before disappearing from the area. Legend tells that the Natives left behind the giant monster in order to protect their history and legacy. When the white pioneers began to permanently settle the area, they, too, began to encounter the unknown beast of the lake.

Rocky: The Rock Lake Terror

Several odd monster sightings occurred in 1867 and were covered in the *Lake Mills Spike* newspaper. Apparently the beast liked to camouflage itself among the weeds of the shoreline, and that is exactly where Mr. R. Hassam, a sharp-eyed witness, spotted the creature lurking. At first glance, Hassam believed it to be nothing but an oddly shaped log. However, on closer inspection "he saw it was a thing of life and struck it with a spear, but could no more hold it than an ox."

On several occasions, the serpent was also spotted by a man named Herbeck, who claimed that not only did the beast hiss at him in a menacingly manner, but that it also swallowed up his fishing bait and yanked his boat through the water with unimaginable strength.

The most captivating sighting occurred in 1882 and was covered in full detail by the *Lake Mills Spike*. While out racing their boats on the lake, Ed McKenzie and D.W Seybert were busy rowing when they caught sight of what appeared to be a large log moving directly in front of them. Without warning, the "log" came to life and opened its huge jaws. The beast simultaneously reared its head a clear three feet out of the water before

Rocky is one of the most infamous Wisconsin lake monsters

Lake Monsters of Wisconsin

diving back under. Immediately, the beast popped back up again near McKenzie's boat, causing Seybert to yell out "strike him with the oar," but McKenzie was so overcome with terror that all his trembling body could do was to call out to shore for help. "Bring a gun, bring a gun, there's a big thing out here," he screamed. Near the docks on shore, a crowd of men heard the dreadful plea for help, prompting Captain Wilson to seize his shotgun and jump into "the swiftest boat" to mount a rescue of the terrified men. Upon arriving at the spot where the beast was last seen, Captain Wilson noticed that the "air all around was heavy with a most sickening odor." Meanwhile on shore, other witnesses were seeing oddly different things in the lake. John Lund claimed that it looked like a man was struggling out in the water, while Ol Hurd, believed it was a huge dog swimming around. Contrasting both of these theories was the belief of the man closest to the action, as McKenzie claimed the beast was "fully as large as his boat" and had somewhat the color of a pickerel.

In 1943, the creature was once again frightening unsuspecting boaters—this time it was a 15-year-old who spotted the monster. In his 1995 book,

Some believe that ancient pyramids are on the bottom of the lake

Rocky: The Rock Lake Terror

Atlantis in Wisconsin, researcher Frank Joseph included a bizarre story about Rocky. It was a hot summer day in July as the teenager was fishing near the drop off in the lake when he noticed a "billowing effect on the surface" of the water as something 10-feet across made its way up from the depths. Within seconds, the thing was in full view, and the young boy could make out a large dark back and torso of the beast. The creature was a stocky 7 or 8 feet in length. The boy waited for the "brownish-black" animal to rear its head out of the water, but instead the beast suddenly descended back into the depths of the lake.

Adding to the mystery of the area is the bold claim by many researchers that several ancient man-made pyramids dwell on the bottom of Rock Lake. Controversial findings by these researchers also hint at a complete village and various other structures down below…just waiting to be discovered. Today, the legends surrounding Rock Lake are well-known both regionally and nationally. Such notoriety has even prompted a local brewery to create a craft beer aptly named "Rocky's Revenge." Perhaps one-day science will finally solve the enigmatic mysteries lurking in Rock Lake, but until that day arrives, grab a bottle of Rocky's Revenge and some scuba gear, and decide for yourself.

Lake Monsters of Wisconsin

Even More Lake Monsters

Not all lake monsters have a long and sorted history complete with decades of bizarre sightings. Often times these unexplainable creatures simply appear for a brief instance. If we are lucky, someone is around to catch a fleeting glace at these elusive beasts. This chapter contains locations around the state where the monsters may have only been seen a couple of times, or cases where additional information is tucked away in some dusty file cabinet just waiting to be discovered—cases that, as of yet, do not warrant an entire chapter. However, the lack of depth in these cases is by no means a measure of their weirdness; as you will soon discover, oddness has no size limitations.

Lake Monsters of Wisconsin

Elkhart Lake Dragon

Where To Encounter It

Elkhart Lake is located in the town of the same name. There are numerous places around the lake for you to experience the dragon.

Creature Lore

Charles Brown wrote of a "probable water dragon" inhabiting Elkhart Lake that dated back to the late 1800s. One morning (no date or year given) a fisherman wandered out to the pier to check a line he had previously attached to the dock. As he began to reel in the heavy duty line, he immediately felt an extremely strong tug—a telltale sign of a true whopper. With much exertion, the fisherman finally managed to lure the beast back toward the pier. Just as the exhausted fisherman was about to land his prize, the beast made one final pull so strong that it sent the fisherman "end over end" into the drink. As he struggled to get his bearings in the water, the fisherman caught sight of the large head of the nearby creature. To make matters worse, the creature's eyes were flashing, and its large sharp jaws were wide open as though it was poised for an attack. Not looking to tempt fate and discover the beast's intentions, the fisherman hastily swam to shore. Apparently, the fisherman's account was so terrifying that it caused a mass exodus of swimmers from the nearby resorts.

Over the years, I have tirelessly searched for more information on the Elkhart Lake Dragon, yet each and every one of my attempts has proven futile. I have scoured local newspapers, spoken with countless residents, pestered the Chamber of Commerce and local historians, and still I've found myself no closer to locating any other documentation of this dragon. I am hoping that someone reading this book will have the missing pieces of this puzzle.

Even More Lake Monsters

Trump Lake Mystery

Where to Encounter It

Trump Lake is approximately 3 miles north of the small northern town of Wabeno.

Creature Lore

A little late to the game, the monster legend of Trump Lake sprung up in May of 1935. Two brothers, F.J. & Robert Kopecky, were out fishing in their small boat, when out of nowhere a large commotion near the shore caught their attention. According to the *La Crosse Tribune*, the "water was churned to waves and the air filled with a whistling sound like a high wind." Whatever was causing the disturbance suddenly made a "large arc out into the lake, churning the water to two foot waves and still emitting the strange sound. It then disappeared." Around town, there was no shortage of explanations; everything from sharks to sea serpents was proposed as viable theories for the commotion. The newspaper reported that many of the old timers in town believed the disturbance had to be caused by a "hungry muskie," or two "fighting pickerel." Interestingly, the newspaper mentioned that a similar incident had occurred on Trump Lake just a few weeks prior to their report.

As is often the case, when I started to research this story I discovered that any remnants of the original legend had all but been lost to history. The local librarian (an invaluable source for any monster researcher) put me in touch with several locals who she thought would have some unique perspective on the lake's history, including some descendants of the original witnesses. One gentleman told me that for the last 60 years he has been spending many summers vacationing at Trump Lake, and had never once heard of any serpent legend. Another local man remembered hearing stories about a fish the size of an oar that would often follow boaters—

Lake Monsters of Wisconsin

but he could add no further details. After sharing the original article with some residents, I had many people exposing theories that paralleled the original explanations. However, one gentleman put a new twist on the case by suggesting that the commotion may have been caused by a methane gas leak in the lake. For now, it looks like the cause of the commotion will continue to be a mystery.

**The next three lakes—Okauchee, Lac La Belle, and Oconomowoc—are all located relativity close to one another. Since many of the legends seemed to group the three together as all having similar reports, the individual stories seem interchangeable. I also include Fowler Lake in this discussion due to its close proximity to these lakes (see the Fowler Lake chapter…also Pewaukee Lake is not far from here either—See Pewaukee Lake). **

Okauchee Lake

Where To Encounter It

Okauchee Lake is located just east of Oconomowoc.

Creature Lore

For years, rumors of a giant beast loose in Okauchee Lake circulated among folklorists and paranormal researchers. Outside of the general overall legend, researchers had limited other details to help substantiate the story, leaving many to assert that it was nothing more than an urban legend. However, I was able to find one piece of information that could add some much needed credibility to the legend of Okauchee. While reading a July 24, 1892 article in the *Chicago Tribune* that described several monsters in southern Wisconsin lakes, I noticed a one sentence report about an actual Okauchee Lake sighting. The article states that during the pre-

Even More Lake Monsters

vious fall (1891) an angler was out spearing fish when he encountered a "buffalo fish" that was over "six feet long." Gauging the overall size of the creature, including scales as large as silver dollars, the fisherman estimated that the beast had to have weighed somewhere between eighty or ninety pounds. If the fisherman did indeed encounter a ninety-pound buffalo fish (*Ictiobus Cyprinellus*) it would have been a new world record. Maybe what the man saw wasn't a buffalo fish…maybe it was the much talked about water beast of the lake. This case illustrates that for many urban legends out there, evidence of their origin is often just a newspaper article away.

Lac La Belle Lake

Where To Encounter It

Lac La Belle Lake is just north of Oconomowoc.

Creature Lore

Much like Okauchee Lake, Lac La Belle Lake is steeped in legend but short on documentation. Although it is listed as having a lake monster in various current books, newspaper articles, and websites, no real documentation is ever cited. The closest research I have found is the abovementioned *Chicago Tribune* article which claimed, "at intervals for a number of years an immense fish" had been seen in La Belle Lake (and others), yet no possible culprits were listed. A popular theory of the time was that a giant beaver or otter lived in the lake, and its huge tail splash was often mistaken for a serpent.

\

Lake Monsters of Wisconsin

The Oconomowoc Lake Demon

Where To Encounter It

Oconomowoc Lake is just southeast of Oconomowoc—right off of Highway 16.

Creature Lore

Just like in the previous two cases, the same *Chicago Tribune* article lists Oconomowoc Lake as having some sort of giant aquatic beast. This time though, Wisconsin Folklorist Charles Brown added some additional details in his 1942 sea serpent monograph. He reported that, in years prior, the Oconomowoc beast was often seen, and it was so terrifying that witnesses referred to as a "demon." One such witness was Anthony Derse, a local judge, who was said to have spun several good stories about the monster.

Lake Kegonsa

Where To Encounter It

Lake Kegonsa is just east of Kegonsa—right off of Highway 51.

Creature Lore

One of the hallmarks of a lake monster is the inherent fear that is generated by their appearance. It only took one sensational sighting to turn an otherwise sleepy resort town into utter turmoil, as curious sight seekers flocked to the water in droves, each possessing the dream of seeing their own prehistoric aquatic dinosaur. Common sense dictates that dangerous close calls with giant sea monsters would act as a deterrent to future boaters and swimmers. Yet, once again, the human fascination with the perilous, the risky, and the precarious appeared to overwrite any pre-programmed fight or flight response. It is that same thought procedure that impels people to climb Mt. Everest or to swim with deadly sharks. Humans are simply drawn to excitement. Although deep down we know that death lurks around every corner, some people simply cannot resist the urge to peek around that corner. Such is the case with the Lake Kegonsa monster. According to Charles Brown, this lake monster, which he dubbed a "dragon," gained a reputation as being more "vengeful" than its contemporaries. According to Brown, those who frequently spotted the beast off of Colladay Point & Williamson Point believed that the beast possessed a "destructive nature."

Unfortunately, like much of Brown's published work on sea serpents, no citations were given for his stories. Folklorists of that time were hell bent on preserving legends that were in critical danger of dying out, and for the most part researchers like Brown made every attempt to legitimize their research through meticulous notes and journals. If Brown did record the origin of these tales, the sources have not been published. After years of searching, scouring, and digging, I was left holding nothing. My pursuit to uncover the truth behind this legend hit the proverbial dead end, and I was forced to accept the fact that no matter how earnest and driven we are in our quest to hold onto legends, superstitions, and folklore, sometimes they are simply washed away by the passing of time. Whatever witnesses Brown spoke with, whatever resorts he staked out, and whatever first-hand accounts he captured, they remain as hidden as the monster he was hunting.

Northport River Monster

Where To Encounter It

The exact whereabouts of this monster are still unknown. My leading theory is that this sighting took place in the Mink River, which sits a few miles south of Northport.

Creature Lore

During July of 1904, James Thorson, an angler from New London, was out fishing on an unnamed river near Northport. According to the *Postville Review,* Thorson sat out on the lake for over two hours without registering one single bite. Then, suddenly, he felt a "tremendous" tug on his line. Whatever was attached to the other end of his line was so powerful that it began pulling Thorson's boat through the water at a tremendous rate. As his boat was water skiing down the river, it finally smashed into a log and overturned, catapulting him into the river. He then "gained the bottom of the boat and paddled to shore with his hands. The pole disappeared down the river." I was able to find the same identical article about Thorson's adventure in several newspapers from around the country. Curiously though, I have not been able to locate any write ups about the incident in any of the Door County newspapers.

Another problem I ran into with this case was the lack of any rivers in the area where the sighting was alleged to have happened. The closet (and only) river near the town of Northport is the Mink River—which is located about 4-5 miles south of town. I did contact several long standing resorts of the area to see if the story rang a bell with them, but no one I spoke with had ever heard of the sighting.

Even More Lake Monsters

The Clear Lake Creature

Where To Encounter It

Clear Lake is located near Milton. There are plenty of public viewing spots, including a public camping resort, right on the lake.

Creature Lore

Just like the main character from the novel *The Curious Case of Benjamin Button*, the Clear Lake serpent legend seems to be operating in reverse. Let me explain. Normally in folklore a legend is born, it progresses, it morphs, and then it dies out and it is inevitably forgotten. But the Clear Lake legend took a different route, because the first time I heard about this legend was through an 1893 article headlined: "Clear Lake Sea Serpent Dead." Until this time, the Clear Lake creature was not on any monster hunter's map—including mine.

Thankfully, the *Janesville Gazette* article provided some background on the legend. Apparently, for years, the good people of Janesville made frequent excursions to Clear Lake with high hopes of seeing the creature. Those hopes were quickly squashed in 1893 by Maud Richardson and Florine Ogden, who noticed the creature "rear its ugly head out of the lake." Apparently these hardcore women were ready for anything because after sighting the creature, the pair hurriedly equipped themselves with clubs, hopped in a boat, and headed off for some monster-killing action. Somehow the women tracked the beast down, and with a "few well directed blows stilled the horrid wrigglings" of the monster. With the carcass in hand, the triumphant ladies rowed their prey back to shore.

Even more amazing than two 1800s women tracking down and killing a sea monster was the fact that the one-paragraph article contained no further details. Was it such an overwhelming news day that the paper couldn't spare a few words to describe what the creature looked like, how the women tracked it, or God forbid, take a photo of a previously unknown species? It is frustrating beyond measure to find such an interesting case, yet have no means of following up on it. If such a thing happened today, you could call the reporter, interview the witnesses, or even wander down and check out the dead creature for yourself. Until that day comes, we are left with this inconclusive story.

The Green Lake Serpent

Where To Encounter It

Green Lake is located in Green Lake and has plenty of public access points for any level of monster hunter.

Creature Lore

Researching the Green Lake serpent is a bit like overhearing someone talking on the cell phone—you only get one side of the story. Two separate one-sentence mentions make up the entirety of written reports that I have found. In 1886, the *Oshkosh Daily Northwestern* dashed the hopes of monster hunters by proclaiming, "The Green Lake sea serpent has retired for the season and taken up quarters in Sandstone Bluff." (Sandstone Bluff is on the southeastern side of the lake.)

One year later, in 1887, after several serpent sightings in Lake Koshkonong (See Koshkonong chapter) the *Oshkosh Daily Northwestern* publically wondered if the Green Lake serpent had "changed quarters?" Obviously, it is difficult to ascertain answers from a combined three sentences of sightings, leaving it to ones imagination as to what occurred to land Green Lake with its serpent reputation.

Even More Lake Monsters

French Lake

Where To Encounter It

French Lake in the northeastern portion of the state—approximately 15 miles southwest of Powell.

Creature Lore

The only mention of a sea monster in the lake came from a 1916 *La Crosse Tribune* article where the writer, while referencing an ill reporter, stated his hope that the reporter will recover in time for the "annual discovery of the sea serpent in French Lake." No other written mentions of this monster have yet been discovered.

Storr's (Storrs) Lake

Where To Encounter It

Storr's Lake is located just east of Milton, off of Highway 26. The lake has a public boat landing for you to start your adventure.

Creature Lore

Imagine traveling out to the nearby lake to escape the stifling summer heat. You have packed a hearty lunch and plenty of beverages to keep you cool as you make your way to your favorite sunning spot—only to discover that something humungous has already beat you to it. That is exactly the bizarre scenario that the people Milton experienced back in 1896. It was a wonderful June day when those at Storr's Lake noticed a gigantic serpent sprawled out along the lake shore. The beast, estimated by witnesses to be well over 100 feet long, was covered in "silvery shiny scales." The stunned witnesses watched as the beast rolled around on the shore for a few moments before it "slipped off into the water and disappeared from sight."

Lake Monsters of Wisconsin

As far as I am aware this is the only reported sighting of something in Storr's Lake. With a span of just over 20 acres, and a maximum depth of 25 feet, it seems highly unlikely that a gargantuan 100-foot monster could dwell in such a small lake while remaining undetected. However, the lake's low clarity and deep water pockets could help keep the creature from any prying eyes1}.

Chain O' Lakes

Where To Encounter It

The Chain O' Lakes is a series of 22 connected lakes near Waupaca. As you can imagine with so many lakes there are countless way to get close to the water.

Creature Lore

American Indian lore tells the cautionary tale of a large water monster (*Ma-Sheno-Mak*) that would grab ahold of people and drag them under to their watery graves. One would be best served to be on full alert while crossing any body of water, lest the monster gobbles you up as well. The Native people living along the shores of the Chain O' Lakes believed that a similar monster was in the lakes as well. Like many oral tales, written documentation of the monster is very rare. In 1913, the *Marshfield Times* gave vague details of about the Chain O' Lakes, writing that the lakes were "safe habitation to a sea-serpent."

I also found a 1937 newspaper article that focused on the Wisconsin Historical Society's research into Native legends. The *Appleton Post-Crescent* mentioned briefly that, for ages, the Natives believed that water monsters dwelled in Chain O' Lakes. Apparently, at an old "Indian crossing" in the lakes, there lived "a water monster who caught unwary Indians who were fording the stream." To help ensure safe passage, and to protect themselves

Even More Lake Monsters

from this deadly monster, offerings of tobacco were often placed on the edge of the water. Which of the 22 lakes had a monster(s) in them has not been determined.

Lake Monsters of Wisconsin

The following places have all surfaced as places with lake monster legends. Often they have appeared on Wisconsin sea serpent lists—with no further details included. I am currently searching for more information to determine the extent of these legends:

Lake Chippewa

Lake Wingra

Milwaukee River

Poygan Lake

Shawano Lake

Yellow River

Bibliography

Case 1 – The Amphibious Demon of Brown's Lake
Burlington Standard April 10, 1876
Burlington Standard July 9, 1976
Racine Journal Times July 14, 1976

Case 2 – Bozho- The Lake Mendota Sea Serpent
Brown, Charles. *Sea serpents; Wisconsin occurrences of these weird water monsters in the Four lakes, Rock, Red Cedar, Koshkonong, Geneva, Elkhart, Michigan, and other lakes.* Wisconsin Folklore Society. 1942
Chicago Tribune July 24, 1892
Eau Claire News October 28, 1892
Janesville Gazette October 6, 1892
Madison Wisconsin State Journal November 1, 1925
Marshfield Times August 30, 1892
Oshkosh Daily Northwestern July 25, 1892
Rath, Jay. *The W-Files: True Reports of Unexplained Phenomena in Wisconsin.* Madison. Wisconsin Trails. 1997.
Racine Daily Journal August 4, 1899

Case 3- Cloverleaf Lakes Creature
Eau Claire Leader August 24, 1910
Janesville Daily Gazette August 22, 1910

Case 4- The Deadly Mississippi River Terror
Dubuque Telegraph Herald July 12, 1910
Eau Claire Leader June 18, 1904
Eau Claire Weekly Telegram August 21, 1902
Elyria Reporter June 4, 1904
La Crosse Daily Press July 20, 1901

Lake Monsters of Wisconsin

La Crosse Tribune January 25, 1921
Lewis, Chad. *Hidden Headlines of Wisconsin*. Eau Claire. On the Road Publications. 2007
Lewis, Chad, Voss, Noah. *Pepie: The Lake Monster of the Mississippi River*. Eau Claire. On the Road Publications. 2014

Case 5- The Denizen of Lake Koshkonong
Brown, Charles. *Sea serpents; Wisconsin occurrences of these weird water monsters in the Four lakes, Rock, Red Cedar, Koshkonong, Geneva, Elkhart, Michigan, and other lakes*. Wisconsin Folklore Society. 1942
Gard, Robert, Sorden, L.G. *Wisconsin Lore*. Madison. Wisconsin House. 1962
Hoard Historical Museum. Telephone Interview. May 2016
Oshkosh Daily Northwestern November 19, 1887

Case 6- The Elusive Beast of Lake Emerson
La Crosse Tribune and Leader Press August 12, 1926
Madison Capital Times July 5, 1939

Case 7- The Fowler Lake Lop Jaw
Cannelton Reporter August 26, 1876
Chicago Tribune July 24, 1892
Waukesha Freeman July 20, 1905

Case 8- The Fox Lake Lurker
Janesville Gazette August 12, 1892
Milwaukee Journal August 1892
Waukesha Freeman August 18, 1892

Case 9 – The Half Moon Monster
Burlington Weekly Hawkeye August 12, 1886

Bibliography

Chippewa Falls Herald September 4, 1891
Eau Claire Daily Free Press July 12, 1886
Eau Claire Daily Free Press July 14, 1886
Eau Claire Daily Free Press July 29, 1886
Eau Claire Daily Leader June 19, 1887
Eau Claire News July 17, 1886
Eau Claire Leader April 20, 1900
Lewis, Chad. *Hidden Headlines of Wisconsin*. Eau Claire. Unexplained Research Publishing Company,. 2007
Oshkosh Daily Northwestern July 26, 1886

Case 10- Jenny, The Lake Monster of Geneva Lake
Chicago Tribune July 24, 1892
Janesville Daily Gazette 1906
Janesville Gazette September 29, 1902
Lake Geneva Herald September 28, 1902
Wisconsin State Journal August 12, 1899
Xenia Daily Gazette August 9, 1892

Case 11 – The Lake Delevan Giant
Green Bay Gazette August, 1902
Janesville Daily Gazette September 10, 1902
Janesville Daily Gazette August 3, 1903
Janesville Daily Gazette August 3, 1906
Madison Journal August, 1902
Marshall Daily News April 8, 1903
Oshkosh Daily Northwestern August 25, 1902
Racine Daily Journal August 25, 1902

Case 12- The Lake Hallie Whopper
Eau Claire Free Press Weekly July 25, 1895

Lake Monsters of Wisconsin

Case 13- The Lake Michigan Leviathan
Boston Post August 1, 1883
Manitowoc Lake Shore Times August 28, 1883
Racine Daily Journal December 20, 1900
Racine Journal July 14, 1903
Racine Journal Times July 29, 1935
Sheboygan Daily Press July 6, 1903
Sheboygan Press July 16, 1936
Weekly Wisconsin November 5, 1887

Case 14 – The Lake Monona Sea Serpent
Janesville Daily Gazette August 24, 1894
Janesville Gazette June 11, 1892
Oshkosh Daily Northwestern July 25, 1892
Rath, Jay. *The W-Files: True Reports of Unexplained Phenomena in Wisconsin.* Madison. Wisconsin Trails. 1997.
Wisconsin State Journal June 12, 1897

Case 15- The Lake Ripley Fright
Chicago Daily Tribune July 19, 1896
Janesville Gazette September, 1891
Janesville Gazette July 19, 1945
Osseo-Eleva Journal 1896
Waukesha Freeman March 9, 1895
Wisconsin State Journal 1945

Case 16 – The Lake Waubesa What's It
Brown, Charles. *Sea serpents; Wisconsin occurrences of these weird water monsters in the Four lakes, Rock, Red Cedar, Koshkonong, Geneva, Elkhart, Michigan, and other lakes.* Wisconsin Folklore Society. 1942

Bibliography

Case 17 – The Lake Winnebago Water Beast

Chicago Tribune July 29, 1891

Gard, Robert, Sorden, L.G. *Wisconsin Lore*. Madison. Wisconsin House. 1962

Milwaukee Weekly Wisconsin July 22, 1889

Oshkosh Daily Northwestern April 14, 1887

Oshkosh Daily Northwestern April 28, 1887

Oshkosh Daily Northwestern November 7, 1895

Oshkosh Daily Northwestern August 20, 1907

San Antonio Daily Light July 22, 1889

Washington Post May 12, 1911

Case 18 – The Long Neck of Long Lake

Benson, Bill. Phone Interview. April 2016

Campbellsport News September 29, 1988

Godfrey, Linda. *Monsters of Wisconsin*. Stackpole Books, June 2011.

Milwaukee Journal September 5, 1989

October 2000. January 5, 2016.

Case 19- The Monster in Devil's Lake

Capital Times July 9, 1964

Chicago Tribune July 11, 1892

Francis, Scott. *Monster Spotter's Guide to North America*. How Books. 2007

Lange, Kenneth, Tuttle, Ralph. *A Lake Where Spirits Live*. 1975

Pillsbury, Diane. Personal Interview. April 2011

Storm, Rory. *Monster Hunt: The Guide to Cryptozoology*. Sterling 2008

Xenia Daily Gazette August 9, 1892

Case 20 – A Mystery in Lake Superior

Detroit News-Tribune 1897

Lake Monsters of Wisconsin

Ironwood News Record August 3,1895

Mayo, William, Barthel, Kate. *The Mysterious North Shore: A Collection of Short Stories About Ghosts, UFOs, Shipwrecks, and More.* Adventure Publications. 2007

Case 21 – Pepie: The $50,000 Lake Monster

"Alien Bigfoot, Cajun Werewolf, Lake Pepin Monster." *Monsters and Mysteries in America*. Destination America. 14 April, 2014. Television.

Durand Courier-Wedge 3 December, 1987.

Freier, Heidi. Telephone and Email Interview. April 2014.

Hennepin, Louis. *A New Discovery of a Vast Country in America.* 1600s.

Heuvelmans, Bernard. *In the Wake of Sea Serpents*. London: Rupert Hart-Davis Ltd. 1968.

Janesville Gazette 24 August, 1867.

Lake City Historical Society. *Lake City, Minnesota Our Historical Journal.* Virginia Beach: The Donning Company Publishers, 2007.

Lewis, Chad. The Wisconsin Road Guide to Mysterious Creatures. Eau Claire: On the Road Publications. 2011.

Nielson, Larry. Personal Interview. September, 2013.

Pierce County Herald. 14 July, 1875

Raymond, Steve. Telephone and Email Interview. April, 2014

Scott, Tom. Telephone Interview. April, 2014

Semi-Weekly Wisconsin. 28 July, 1875.

Stone, Chuck. Telephone Interview. April, 2014

"The Monster of Lake Pepin." *Life to the Max.* WCCO-TV. 31 October, 2009. Television.

Wabasha Daily Sentinel 26 April 1871.

Case 22- The Pewaukee Lake Intruder

Brown, Charles. *Sea serpents; Wisconsin occurrences of these weird*

Bibliography

water monsters in the Four lakes, Rock, Red Cedar, Koshkonong, Geneva, Elkhart, Michigan, and other lakes. Wisconsin Folklore Society. 1942

Racine Journal Times Sunday Bulletin July 11, 1971

Case 23- Red Cedar Lake Monster
Brown, Charles. *Sea serpents; Wisconsin occurrences of these weird water monsters in the Four lakes, Rock, Red Cedar, Koshkonong, Geneva, Elkhart, Michigan, and other lakes.* Wisconsin Folklore Society. 1942
Janesville Gazette September 5, 1891
Marshfield Times August 24, 1894
Oshkosh Daily Northwestern August 15, 1890
Pocahontas County Sun June 16, 1892
Waterloo Daily Courier May 9, 1892

Case 24 – The Rock River Visitor
Beaver Dam Daily Citizen October 15, 2005
Janesville Daily Gazette September 21, 1903
Janesville Gazette February 19, 1892
Madison Capital Times September 7, 1940
Wisconsin State Journal July 30, 1950

Case 25 – Rocky, The Rock Lake Inhabitant
Joseph, Frank. *Atlantis in Wisconsin: New Revelations About the Lost Sunken City.* Galde Press 1995.
Lake Mills Spike August 31, 1882

Case 26- Even More Lake Monsters
Elkhart Lake Dragon
Brown, Charles. *Sea serpents; Wisconsin occurrences of these weird water monsters in the Four lakes, Rock, Red Cedar, Koshkonong,*

Lake Monsters of Wisconsin

    Geneva, Elkhart, Michigan, and other lakes. Wisconsin Folklore Society. 1942

Trump Lake Mystery

    La Crosse Tribune May 27, 1935

Okauchee Lake

    Chicago Tribune July 24, 1892

Lac La Belle Lake

    Chicago Tribune July 24, 1892

The Oconomowoc Lake Demon

    Brown, Charles. Sea serpents; Wisconsin occurrences of these weird water monsters in the Four lakes, Rock, Red Cedar, Koshkonong, Geneva, Elkhart, Michigan, and other lakes. Wisconsin Folklore Society. 1942

    Chicago Tribune July 24, 1892

Lake Kegonsa

    Brown, Charles. Sea serpents; Wisconsin occurrences of these weird water monsters in the Four lakes, Rock, Red Cedar, Koshkonong, Geneva, Elkhart, Michigan, and other lakes. Wisconsin Folklore Society. 1942

Northport River Monster

    Postville Review July 29, 1904

The Clear Lake Creature

    Janesville Gazette August 25, 1893

The Green Lake Serpent

    Oshkosh Daily Northwestern October 2, 1886

    Oshkosh Daily Northwestern November 19, 1887

French Lake

    La Crosse Tribune February 2, 1916

Storr's (Storrs) Lake

    Milwaukee Weekly Wisconsin June 27, 1896

Chain O' Lakes

    Appleton Post-Crescent November 1, 1937

    Marshfield Times November 26, 1913

Author Bio

Chad Lewis

For over two decades Chad Lewis has traveled the back roads of the world in search of the strange and unusual. From tracking vampires in Transylvania and searching for the elusive monster of Loch Ness to trailing the dangerous *Tata Duende* through remote villages of Belize and searching for ghosts in Ireland's haunted castles, Chad has scoured the earth in search of the paranormal.

Chad has been featured on the *Discovery Channel's A Haunting, William Shatner's Weird or What, ABC's Scariest Places on Earth, Monsters and Mysteries in America*, along with being a frequent contributor on *Ripley's Believe it or Not Radio*. With a Master's Degree in Psychology, Chad has authored over 20 books on the supernatural, and extensively lectures on his fascinating findings. The more bizarre the legend, the more likely it is that you will find Chad there.